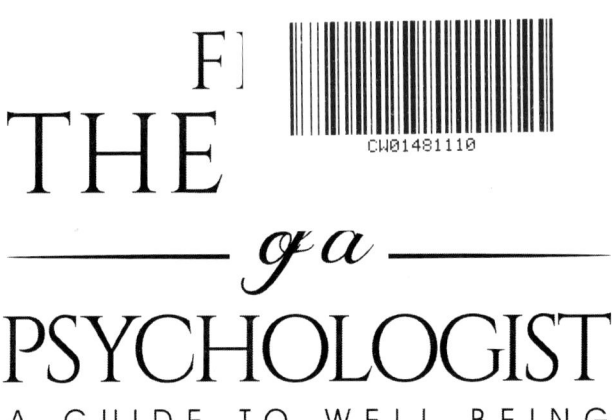

THE F] ~~CW01481110~~

of a

PSYCHOLOGIST

A GUIDE TO WELL BEING

Dr. Asha Dinesh

INDIA · SINGAPORE · MALAYSIA

Notion Press

Old No. 38, New No. 6
McNichols Road, Chetpet
Chennai - 600 031

First Published by Notion Press 2019
Copyright © Dr. Asha Dinesh 2019
All Rights Reserved.

ISBN 978-1-68466-342-2

Dedication

To my parents,

For their deep love

For allowing me to be myself.

To Dinesh and Karan,

For their immense love and support

Which helped me become a better version of myself.

Contents

Contents

Foreword

I feel proud to write the foreword to this remarkably well-written book entitled *From The Diary Of A Psychologist - A Guide To Well-Being.* Actually, I am reminded of the book *Letters from a Father to His Daughter* written by the first Prime Minister of Independent India, Pandit Shri Jawaharlal Nehru. Though this book may appear to be of fiction value, it is definitely based on the rich professional experience of the author Dr. Asha Dinesh, who has come out with a lot of interesting facts that she has so dearly collected and documented.

I am all the more happy that Dr. Asha Dinesh, who did her doctoral research at the Department of Psychology in the University of Madras with my guidance in the early 1990s, is meticulously doing her professional service to society ever since she became a fully qualified psychologist with a Ph.D. in Psychology awarded to her in 1994.

Many in the modern world either think that psychology is sheer common sense or use psychology interchangeably with psychiatry. Both are inexcusably wrong. The human mind is so complex that one cannot always proceed with common sense. A thorough understanding of the mind will be possible only when individuals are seen professionally from various possible angles across different points of time using a variety of techniques such as observations, interviews, and questionnaires. These form a part of the case study approach.

The first wave of psychotherapy concentrated heavily on past experiences, and it was problem centric. Theoretically, it was quite sound. The second wave which followed also had a sound theoretical base and it was in a way past-oriented but present was its main focus. The third wave took a slightly different path. **The third wave continues to concentrate on the present but with a future orientation.** It does not seem to worry much about causes, but it is determined to provide viable solutions by concentrating on residual resources (till left intact despite pathology) or basic competencies with which one is born.

The fourth wave emphasizes the importance of compassion by advocating the maintenance of dignity, forgiveness, and gratitude, all of which have strong connotations with overall well-being. Dr. Asha has borne this vital point (fostering well-being) in mind while writing this book which is bound to enlighten the readers especially parents.

She has structured this book very neatly with five finely interrelated parts namely [i] individuality and illuminating factor, [ii] a perfect connect - the precise need, [iii] attention – a therapeutic tool and [iv] a word on parenting and [v] dealing with emotions - distinctive way of handling situations.

The main aim of the author in writing this book is to bring each and every individual close to reality by matching the inner world consisting of several personality traits with the external world which is full of challenges and opportunities. I sincerely hope that society in general and families, in particular, enjoy the fruits of technology with overall well-being.

– Dr. V.D. Swaminathan,

Professor, Department of Psychology,

University of Madras

Preface

*F*rom *the diary of a psychologist is the essence of my two decades of practice as a psychotherapist. Here I have chosen to address the most common issues for which individuals seek the help of a psychologist both personal and interpersonal. Beginners of psychotherapy will be able to understand the nuances of psychological concepts in a very simplified fashion. As a therapist, I have always felt that these concepts need to be taken to the common man so that he can apply them in every sphere of his life.*

I have incorporated my experience in private practice, prisons, remand homes, hospital, and factories. I have also attempted to answer some of the common questions asked in workshops, public meetings, and seminars.

I have attempted to demonstrate very crucial psychological concepts in a very simplified form. There is a child in all of us who is interested in stories, and hence I have used the case study method to make these concepts clear.

Preface

The objective of this book is to understand one's own beliefs which can be a major barrier and can also lead to major growth in one's self as well as in relationships. The first part is exclusively on the self as I strongly believe that the growth of the self only can lead to growth in relationships and other spheres. This is followed by skills to deal in interpersonal relationships at the personal and professional front to bring about harmony for the self and relationships.

This is the first volume of the series. The following volumes will focus on other crucial areas.

The names and identities in the cases have been completely changed on the account of confidentiality and professional ethics.

The idea for this book sparked when I wrote A Letter to My Son. This was a small booklet I wrote for my son who was stepping into adulthood when he turned twenty-one. His response to this letter was of immense value, and he said it would help him as a guide in his life. I wanted to translate similar concepts into a book which would help readers understand their life better. Lots of self-introspection happened spontaneously as this book evolved, which helped me as an individual and also as a psychologist.

Acknowlededements

First and foremost I seek pleasure in expressing my deep gratitude to Dr. V. D. Swami Nathan, my mentor, for his incredible feedback and suggestions on this book. Feedback from an expert like him meant a great deal.

I thank Dr. Balasubramanian, who stood beside me not only as the book evolved but throughout my career as a practicing psychologist. I am highly indebted to you, and I salute your commitment, sir.

I thank my friend, Vijaya Lakshmi Kathirvel, who was the first reader of the manuscript for her enthusiasm, support, and encouragement. Her feedback took my enthusiasm to a higher level.

I thank Mr. Vishal Agarwal for offering his valuable comment.

I thank Mr. Sampath Kumar for dedicating his valuable time and expertise in helping me fine tune the work.

Acknowlededements

I wish to wholeheartedly pay my regards to my friend, Judy Enoch, for her valuable feedback.

I would like to present my warm thanks to my husband, Dinesh and son, Karan for their constant encouragement and support. They took care of my other responsibilities so that I could complete this book comfortably.

I wish to give my special thanks to my team of psychologists, Dr. Sangeetha, Mrs. Jothimathi, Mrs. Sasikala, and Mrs. Manjula. Discussions with them gave me better clarity on my work.

I extend my sincere thanks to my family and friends for their moral and emotional support.

My sincere gratitude to team of Notion Press, especially Ms. Mathanghee for making the entire process of publication very comfortable.

PART - 1

Individuality – An Illuminating Factor

Chandra was seated in front of me sobbing and crying aloud in between. She has gotten married a few weeks back. Her parents had brought her, and the issue is that she is non cooperative with her husband and the marriage has not been consummated.

The mother continues that if the marriage is not made to consummate, Chandra will be sent back and the entire family will have no other go but to commit suicide. Chandra was very helpless, and she was sobbing and narrating the situation. She said that, as a child, all the decisions regarding her dresses, friends she should speak to, school courses, and selection of college was made by her mother. The parents were holding on tight by the neck, and an often heard sentence from the parents was that they know what is good for her. The lines between her and her parents were completely blurred. She was even afraid to express her personal feelings, bothering about the aftermath and the consequences.

She never spoke against their wishes as she believed that it was a sin to oppose her parents. She said parents always wore magnifying glasses to see the mistakes she made. Her fear of committing mistakes grew more and more. As a result, she started relying only on them for every decision. She could not assert herself to anybody now.

When it came to her marriage, her parents had their own criteria for a groom. When she first saw the boy, her feeling towards him was that he was more of a brother and she could not relate to him as a romantic partner. Although she tried her best, she could not evoke that kind of feeling towards him. Although she had hinted to them about her feelings, they had already made up their mind to get her married to him. She was told that all the relatives had already been informed, and nothing could be done. They told her there was no way but to agree for the marriage. Her parents felt that if she gets married into this family, they would have more respect in society.

She tried to call the groom to express her feelings but all in vain. Now that everybody was already informed, he felt he could not do anything.

Amidst this turmoil, she got married. Now that she is married, the same feelings continue. Every day her fear and anxiety are becoming more and more. There is pressure from all the directions to consummate the marriage. The more the pressure, the more her anxiety is becoming uncontrollable. Now the situation is such that the very presence of her husband causes panic.

She was pleading to be rescued from the chaos.

"The greatest prison that people live in is the fear of what other people think."

— David Icke

As an ardent practitioner of psychology, I have observed in my decades of practice, the quantum of space a person allot to others around him in his brain. *This territory in the individual brain which is of the concerned individual; if it is pledged,* the concerned individual thinks and perceives to satisfy each and everyone, losing his originality. The individual becomes conscious or even over conscious, thinking about others, what they may say, or what they would say. He tends to think more about other people, who react to his actions... The comments they would air, or the flatteries and the appreciations they would make on various parameters of his life.

I come across many people who have literally become slaves due to the fear of rejection... And they lose themselves to the praises or approval of those around. Over-consciousness leads to dangerous debacles. Through dependency or over dependency on these external remarks, we practically adorn a façade or false mask to satisfy or please others to receive bouquets and appreciations. We sell ourselves, in reality, to earn appreciations from others.

Leaning to satisfy only others' views loses one's individuality. It is a very huge price we are paying to receive approval from others. In the process, in the majority of the decisions that the person makes in his life, the focus is not himself but those around him. Psychologically, this is the single biggest cause of most unhappiness.

In my experience with the factory workers, I came across a women, Maragatham, who was getting a salary of Rs. 8000/- per month. She found it too difficult to make ends meet. She paid a heavy toll for pleasing others. When her daughter hit puberty, listening to others, she spent lavishly to organize a grand party for all her friends and relatives, borrowing a huge loan of Rs. 50000. Now she is struggling to pay the interest for the loan which she has taken, and she has had to cut her routine monthly household expenses to accommodate this interest payment.

Just for satisfying others, she had to pay a heavy bill through her nose. Curtailing her basic necessities for survival to get appreciations from others for the party offered, she has worsened her own lifestyle and overburdened herself.

Many of us resort to faking and overburdening ourselves. Many of our decisions, like buying a bigger house, buying bigger vehicles, and buying costlier gadgets are to seek social approval. Everybody wants to show others his fake self through different ways. This is an epidemic, and certainly, it leads to self-burdening.

In many of these episodes, the focus is on others. By pleasing others, we lose the connection with the self, and as a result, lose our decision making and identity.

In every human being, there is an original personality without any mask. We come across people who are similar to us in life. In contrast, we pretend to be different. The more the difference between the real self and the pretended self, the more the stress. Moreover, we attract people who are like the false self of us.

On the contrary, people who eulogized and liked your pretend personality would go away from you the moment you stop pretending.

This is commonly seen when it comes to marriage. The eligible brides pretend and be nice to one and all in the family. They become completely artificial to come up to the expectations of everybody. But in reality, the projection of the false self pushes her to the back seat. She obviously wants her original personality to be revealed in its full dimension. But if that is done, and she removes the false mask, people may dislike her. Her problems would become perennial and perpetual after the marriage, as all the concerned relatives search for the initial pretended version of the bride, who impressed them before the marriage.

In most of the cases, we show a different person as we wish to please people... The pleased people compliment us to move towards a euphoric level of life.

Due to this, we are not able to develop a connection with anyone who is like our original self.

Even when a girl says an honest fact about her likes and dislikes, many people are unhappy about it. But there will be people who understand her true self.

During the courtship period, couples only exhibit the best in themselves to their partner. Both of them get more and more fascinated and attracted to the person through the illusion. Once they are married, their real self comes into existence and is openly visible. This disillusioned phase is a critical period of adjustment and compatibility. In many cases, a lot of rifts and conflicts develop during this phase.

A girl may be wearing power glasses, which she has not revealed to her would be husband. When he comes to know about this fact, after the marriage, it may impact the feeling of romance between them as he has to adapt to the new aspect of the person.

There are times when the person getting married is on regular medication for a particular ailment, and when they hide this fact from their better half, the person is forced to continue to hide the medication. This becomes a tiresome source of stress to the person who is hiding this secret and to the life partner. This would persistently be present in the mind of the person who is hiding the fact, and the sense of guilt would prevail, affecting smooth movement with the better half. Actually, such small things like the hiding of particular vital information leads to a lack of trust.

Undoubtedly, such small facts would irritate the relationship. All the partners should understand that they are not going to progress in their relationship by the maintenance of such secrets which are bound to come in open in routine life. This may be a major obstacle in the smooth functioning of a relationship.

Self-Liberation Which Shapes the Person

"To be nobody but yourself in a world which is doing its best night and day to make you everybody else means to fight the hardest battle which any human being can fight."

— *E.E Cummings*

At some point of time, a self-liberation process is required, and it starts happening when you shed the fake self. When I say self-liberation, I do not mean radical individualism or something which is antagonistic to society or a society of one. Self-liberation is about developing and bonding with yourself, which leads to self-fulfillment. When you are connected to the self, and the feelings you feel are absolute completeness, you do not need somebody else's attention to fulfill you. When this happens, there is a feeling of security and comfort within yourself which leads to a feeling of security and comfort with everyone.

To be your true authentic self and have the courage to be YOU, requires you to listen to the feelings which are highly informative. It is to let go of who and what we tell ourselves we SHOULD be and BE what we truly are. This authenticity allows true freedom of self and connection. When we live in this space, it allows us to expose our raw selves and thereby have better compassion for ourselves, and as a result, we are able to have compassion for others.

It is very difficult and tough to find a real you, by 'extinguishing yourself'. It is a phenomenal process to shed the masks which we have been wearing for years. Such a transition is very difficult as we come across numerous hindrances in the process.

I have met numerous people becoming persistently ill with terrible pain and major regrets of not living their life for themselves. Most of the time the need to hide true self is self-inflicted, which is learned from childhood, and which may not actually be expected by others.

Allow your fake self to leave you. While leaving, it is sharing life's lessons with you. Just listen to what it says. Lend your heart to understand what is it conveying to you and what are the guidelines it is conveying to you. Is it asking and directing you to remove all the artificial masks and be your own self?

To be mindful of your true self without judgment is very crucial and critical. Observe situations when you are holding yourself. Vividly understanding and getting in touch with your feelings is thoroughly important. When we do this, we become mindful of the belief that has its grip on us and which is thwarting and restricting us. Most of the time, the cost that is paid in pretending is very high. Being your original self does not mean you will not have any bumps in the road. But when you are in alignment with your soul, you will be steered in the best possible way.

I would like to discuss a person by name. Prabhu, who had incurred a heavy loss in business and had a lot of debt to be settled. He used to tell those people that he would pay their dues in a few days. He gradually developed the habit of avoiding going out on the day he had promised to pay the debt.

As this was incessant, it had a psychological toll on his mind and health. Over a period of time, he avoided going out of the home, fearing debtors. His wife, Ramashri, was very stressed as Prabhu was not able to work and earn. She decided to put an end to it.

Ramashri persisted and motivated Prabhu to come along with her and meet the debtors in person. Both of them went together and informed the debtors that the only way for Prabhu to repay all the debts was by restarting his business.

They assured them that their money would be properly repaid, once his business picked up. They categorically implied to all the concerned debtors that the recouping of the resources would take some time. Although there was a lot of unpleasantness expressed by the debtors verbally, Prabhu and Ramashri were relieved and were able to borrow sufficient time.

That proved to be a much better method than absconding from the debtors, creating much more insecurity about their money. The couple realized the debtors were becoming more and more volatile and aggressive due to their abstaining. But they went and informed them about the practical difficulties and assured the debtors that their dues would be settled once things became better. This self-disclosure helped him to unmask himself.

Knowing the Boundaries and Knocking in the Harmony

"When you feel yourself becoming angry, resentful, or exhausted, pay attention to where you haven't set a healthy boundary."

— Crystal Andrus

A bridegroom, Mr. Srivatsan, was on the verge of marrying a potential bride, Miss. Vardhini, who was also employed. Immediately after getting consent to get married, he informed her that his family was close-knit and they didn't have any secrets between them. Vardhini agreed to her fiancée's words. Slowly, this condition of not keeping secrets mounted to all angles. It even resulted in maintaining confidential bank accounts. Srivatsan insisted that their account would be a joint account for the purpose of transparency. Though initially, he was not talking about restrictions and the limiting of the expenditures, Srivatsan had an eye on Vardhini's expenses. This displeased and annoyed her as his close monitoring of her accounts went to the level of advising her and almost disallowing her to spend her own money. This obviously resulted in a lot of misunderstanding between them, day after day.

The fact which we find from this is that Vardhini was not at all convinced about the idea of a joint account right from the beginning and she was afraid to speak her mind as she felt it would affect the marriage proposal itself. Feeling that the consequences may be bad, she didn't reject the idea of a joint account at the first instance itself. As she was not able to get clarity of thought on this issue or any other matter, she lost her original self, and she presented a confused and blurred picture of herself.

Many times, fearing to talk openly at the right time only evokes confusion at a later stage, causing a total debacle. Many issues are better off cleared in the bud if we properly think. Knowingly many individuals are exhibiting a false self, thinking that they are satisfying others. This results in the brutal assassination of one's original character and also chaos in relationships.

Allowing things to slip away from our control is not going to open up the right way for a comfortable future. Peripheral issues which have accumulated only cause deep concerns during the wide passage of time. And in many scenarios, the original wrong decision becomes very insignificant in the end. As other subsequent blunders are blown out of proportion, the showing of the real face at the right time doesn't happen, and that puts the individuals in an awkward position over a period of time.

Children are not allowed to take or make their own decisions, as they are bound by elders. The children invariably fear the punishments that may follow actions, which the elders may not like. But adults have the liberty in reality and are permitted to take their own decisions, as they have sufficient power and an array of choices.

Here, the awareness of *'boundaries'* has to be implemented. Each and every individual's boundaries are fixed after a total self-analysis of the inner self, which is created by the nucleus of inner consciousness. Boundaries are psychological constructs, although not visible, they make a huge difference in the life of an individual.

Personal boundaries are the limits we set for ourselves as individuals in our interpersonal relationships, both in our personal and professional lives. It helps us guard against being overwhelmed by the demands and fears of others in interpersonal relationships. It protects the inner core of our identity and make us consciously aware of the availability of choice and making use of these choices where ever required.

Boundaries enhance personal psychological space and are highly instrumental in being very clear with one's life with regard to making decisions and taking initiatives.

Our analytical power stands at a supreme high as we know our physical, financial, moral, or practical values to be precise.

Each person knows and understands his own capacity and what he or she can do. How much of anything will be optimum and what will start adding up to pressure. The BOUNDARIES depend exactly on this self-power and self-realization. This fixing of the boundaries clearly sketches the comfort zone psychologically. These deciphered BOUNDARIES clearly reveal 'who we are really' and 'what are the real virtues of our original self'. It gives better clarity to others about us and hence enhances connections and bonding.

The individual originality and identity get lost once we miss out our fixed boundaries. If we take our own determined boundaries as the omnipotent parameters of our own selves, then it is quite obvious that everything is within us. If BOUNDARIES are properly set, the errors, mistakes, blunders, and blemishes may not even exist…

But invariably, we cross our best and ideal guidelines for our boundaries. We cross them when we are making decisions to satisfy some other person. Immersing or submerging our boundaries, we travel on their route and become the reason for total confusion at a later stage. Getting amalgamated with others erases our boundaries and our own identity and individuality.

This type of yielding make us vulnerable. The fixing of boundaries is the best protective skill from stress arising out of interpersonal relationships. That fixation of perfect boundaries only determines our execution of each situation and ultimately all of life. This does not mean that you won't perform anything for anybody. It only means you have your own choices and limitations and you would make a conscious decision for which you may not have to regret.

A sense of comfort and protection comes to those who are able to clearly identify their boundaries. The fixing of boundaries and clearly working with them makes us a real personality, and the model is taken as a convinced pattern for living a true life. It is a real challenge to adhere to this model which is determined by boundaries. But as elders, it would be much easier for us to work out this, compared to our childhood.

Forgetting our boundaries or not even bothering to decipher our own boundaries results in losing one's self. Physically and psychologically, an individual becomes weak due to imagined or real external pressure.

Setting boundaries is not to keep other people out, but it is about keeping you fenced and protected. It is a method of self-care.

Assertive people occupy the pedestal
I care about me too

History and research have proven that the most successful people are clear and assertive and they have a definite idea about their boundaries. People with a strong frame of mind obviously work within their fittest boundaries, and they are proven to have a perfect relationship with all. The honest fact is that these people are appreciated as genuine, straightforward, transparent, and ideal personalities to emulate.

Shobhit is a professional in a private firm and his spouse, Sanchana, was working in the same company as the HR manager. Despite the fact that they work for the same company, rarely do they get time for mutual interaction to upgrade their married life. As weekdays are robbed by official work, they decide to spend their weekends exclusively for themselves and for each other. They firmly decide to care about each other during weekends without bothering about official schedules. They plan to go for movies, dinners, and other outings. On some weekends, they decide to relax at home, enjoying the comfort of each other without any other outdoor activity.

When this was going on, Shobhit's mother-in-law, and Sanchana's mother, Bharathi, who was working and living alone in a neighboring state, on a transfer, moved down to the city where Shobhit and Sanchana were living. Though she initially stayed separately, she preferred to stay with Sanchana and Shobhit. On the weekends, all three of them would be at home. The presence of Bharathi caused a lot of discomfort for Shobhit and Sanchana. Their intercommunication suffered a jolt due to Bharathi's advent. Their privacy was stolen due to the third person's presence in the midst of their home.

The agendas of other people affecting us is a common phenomenon in human life. Yielding to pressure to accommodate others causes these type of debacles in life. His mother-in-law, Bharathi, may not have a clue why Shobhit and Sanchana are irritated, and she will land up mindreading which may add to the confusion.

Most of us really wish to show our original self, but we feel compelled to sport a false face which we assume will be liked by others. Here, the BOUNDARIES come into play and planning or fixing your boundaries needs a lot of self-analysis.

During my initial days of practice as a psychologist, my clients needed short discussions through the phone. Slowly I felt it started consuming more and more of my personal time. There was a time where I had to self-introspect and arrive at my professional boundaries with regard to when and how frequently they can call. This helped my clients and me too. Imagine if these boundaries were not set. It would have reflected on my relationship with them.

This decision making power and taking a definite stance is an essential and vital aspect of each and every one of us. As this is the factor that is going to protect us from feeling claustrophobic in the relationship, clear self-analysis is needed again.

Here is a case of a software professional, Bindu, aged 35. She is a proven workaholic, and she was working on a complex project on her own. But all her colleagues took advantage of her workaholic nature and expected her to do their work also. They would give her flatteries as the price for that. Unable to say 'no' to their face, she stayed late in the office. People assumed that she could stay late and take up more work.

She took work from everybody, resulting in a lot of tension and stress for her. More and more stress and tension practically tortured her. In the process, she went home late, slept late, and woke up late. She had absolutely no time left for herself and her family which created a lot of guilt in her. This piled up stress and pressure erupted out as uncontrollable anger at people around her. Unable to tolerate her anger, people started keeping away from her. It's a paradox that the thirst to be liked by people, in fact, pushes people away.

Here what has actually happened is, each time she agreed to help somebody by going out of the way, she experienced stress, and with this accumulated stress, she turned boisterous and explosive towards herself and towards others.

If she had worked out a strong self-analysis on her limitations and taken precaution in the initial stage itself by setting perfect limits which were healthy for her and also others, so much damage would not have happened.

On the contrary, Nikhil is also in the same rank. He has made his life very balanced. His stance is very clear. He stays only during office hours. He puts in his best and completes his work. He has made it clear to his teammates that he will not stay after office hours. If any meetings are to be scheduled, he will be available only if it is during that time. He will not stretch himself and change his agenda for the sake of others. He has a lot of time left for himself to do his personal work and also for recreation.

He is able to work out, sleep on time, spend time with family, and as a result, there is a lot of satisfaction about life as a whole. This mental well-being leads to better performance and becomes a vicious cycle.

Here, although the output is the same, the difference in the quality of life is because of the boundaries, they set for themselves and others. Bindu feels it is ruthless and selfish to say no to someone asking for help with work. In the process, she is overburdening herself and being ruthless to herself.

Unless we categorically decide to what extent we can help others, it is difficult to lead a peaceful life. Striking a balance is what needed here, and it is imperative that our resources permit us to work for others.

We would have spent a large part of our time and resources trying to meet other people's expectations, to have everyone like us... But when we do this, we are usually out of synchronization with our own wants and needs. This leads to a lot of burnouts in the long run, draining countless energy from us.

To be aware that you have a choice, whether to agree, disagree or partially agree, should be utilized in the right way to have the right type of life. It is the choice which becomes decision making power, which defines our individuality.

Our self-esteem goes up when we master our decisions and take responsibility for them. Philosopher and writer Tariq Ramadan says, "If you do not have a boundary, you do not have a path."

A client of me, Mrs. Rajam, was telling me repeatedly that she is used as a doormat by her family members. Close interaction with the family and a total study and analysis about her revealed she was the culprit and no one else. She allowed everybody to barge into her time and others thought it was okay for her. Her hunger to be NICE was very high, leading to problems in interpersonal relationships.

It is the same as school bullies picking on the smaller and weaker to assert control. They might not bully a person who is confident and who can assert himself. Similar things can happen in work and family scenarios. Bosses may dominate and abuse a subordinate who is more vulnerable just for the sake of scapegoating. This kind of bullying can give them a feeling of power.

Bosses may prey on subordinates who can be a scapegoat to carry their frustrations, just for the sheer pleasure of exercising power.

Like a moth attracted to a flame, passive and docile behavior attracts aggressive and dominant behavior from people. It is very common to hear from people why they are coming across such bullies everywhere. That is why I say the doormat concept is self-inflicted. It needs to be self-introspected on and worked on. A single NO can be the most empowering word if you are in an abusive relationship.

Children who are brought up by controlling, abusive, and neglectful parents often re-experience similar emotions which they have experienced as a child in various settings like at home, work, in the community, and also in romantic relationships.

Boundaries can't be light and loose

The fixing of limits is a highly sensitive and sensible issue. Perfect boundary fixing would make you feel safe and much more comfortable in life.

On the other hand, setting rigid boundaries may chase people from you, and you may feel deprived physically and emotionally. Rigid boundaries are like electric fencing, and it is related to domestic violence or physical abuse, including sexual abuse in the case of children or adults.

If our boundaries are soft, light, and loose, we are permeable to play into other's hands, and we land ourselves in more and more trouble and precarious situations. Hence it is highly important to go through a complete self-analysis and ascertain what type of boundaries would make us really comfortable in leading a powerful life, making everybody around understand us with clarity.

It is really essential and very important to perceive that a lot of time, whether the boundaries we fix are perfect or not, we should also ensure these boundaries do not encroach on our special and quality time. The diplomatic way is to spend considerable time in deciding on these boundaries, but a very clear fact is that if we work without limits and boundaries, we would certainly end up in a mess time and again.

Children in their growing years, when introduced to this concept, learn to respect themselves and respect others. Here is the case of a boy, Rajesh, who is a school goer in high school. He is very fragile, fearful, passive, and docile. He has great difficulty speaking up for himself. All of a sudden he stopped going to school and his parents, Ramu and Susheela, went to the extent of forcing him to go to school.

This made Rajesh abscond from home and attempt suicide. As his mother, Susheela, sought professional help, Rajesh was traced, and after comforting and cajoling him, I had a one on one conversation with him. He revealed the reasons for fleeing from home. His seniors were sexually abusing him. At the first instance,

Rajesh feared them and became a party to their abuse. Day by day, these seniors crowded and molested him as a gang. This was continuing day in and day out. And the persistence of the elder boys went beyond a level, and Rajesh had no outlet to let the secret out.

If somebody would have listened to him patiently and guided him to be firm in dealing with the senior boys, things wouldn't have been so bad, pushing him to the brink of committing suicide.

In such cases, allowing in the maiden trip only causes flutter and abuses. It is only the maiden trip where an individual has a say, and thereafter whatever is tolerated, continues. Such vulnerability is taken advantage of by the miscreants and abusers to exploit the weaker ones. If a strong and stern decision is taken on the first instance, things may not become worse. Allowing children to know about abuse at a tender age and how to deal with such precarious situations is very crucial.

Here, rigid boundaries would only protect an individual from getting abused. Resisting those vulnerabilities should be taught to children. It will make sure that the ordeal won't be repeated.

"The world is in greater peril from those who tolerate or encourage evil than from those who actually commit it."

— Albert Einstein

One is able to set healthy limits only if he is clear of his needs, likes, and dislikes. Even the smallest attempt to accommodate others' likes and dislikes would land the concerned person in definite trouble. Either saying YES without the manipulation of mind or uttering NO without feeling guilty carves one's real personality with individuality.

The eminent psychologist, B.F. Skinner, conducted an experiment with pigeons. He designed a special keyboard. When the pigeon pressed a key of a particular color, a food pallet was released. When some other keys were pressed, the pigeon received a rude shock. Initially, the pigeons pressed the keys randomly, but later, through trial and error, it identified the key which released the food pallet.

Skinner related this to human behavior and showed that behavior which is rewarded will be strengthened for frequent occurrence.

Most abuses, domestic violence, and sexual harassment is rewarded in the maiden trip, and from there, it continues to the level of helplessness. *What you allow is what will continue.*

Knowingly or unknowingly, we reward the behavior of others, which is not acceptable by us. For example, after marriage, if either of the spouses gets involved in abusive behavior and if he or she realizes it pays, it is very likely that this behavior will continue. Often rewarding people's manipulation results in them in becoming more manipulative.

When a child understands that his mother completes all his work when he is not well, he or she tries to manipulate this to shirk their own responsibilities and commitments

Stressing boundaries are created only to protect and safeguard one's individuality. They are the part of our self-care and well-being. They are clear, protective, and not harmful. They are appropriate and very essential. It is always you who has to curtail or expand boundaries to whomever concerned. Healthy limits help us to grow in perfect dimensions.

Umbilical cord- the right time to detach

When I started my practice, it was very difficult to connect theory with the practical. In each and every case, I came across a lot of doubts and queries. I had to depend on my mentor and guide, Dr. Swaminathan, who is a proven expert in dealing with clinical psychological issues. His spontaneous suggestions only kept me going and making me learn the nuances of the sphere in the fittest sense of it.

Calling Dr. Swaminathan after each and every counseling became a routine for me, and I was not able to resist the temptation of talking to him at least once during each case study. I knew it was embarrassing and delicate for him, but I had no other go but to talk to him to arrive at a better direction of counseling for a given case. Resorting to his advice was imperative for me to feel more confident as a professional. But at some point of time, when a client came, I sought the advice of Dr. Swaminathan. He reverted back to me pertinently, about what I would do if I had to handle the case with my own perceptions. I analyzed it and replied. He was happy and glad with my answer and informed me and appreciated me with a single word, PERFECT.

He further added that this was the right time to stick to my own decisions on each and every case I handled. He gave me the confidence that I can handle any sensitive case on my own, without his support. He further enunciated that it was high time that I establish my own practice individually. At that point, he illustrated that at some point of time, the UMBILICAL CORD has to be detached.

Honestly, I felt it was a jolt for my thinking. Dr. Swaminathan would always be there to guide me in my practice for a lifetime. But his decision became a blessing to me. I had to have a lot of cross-fertilization of ideas within me while analyzing the cases with the proper perspective.

This made me come out with result oriented perfect suggestions. It brought out the fullest potential within me.

And due to the timely judgment of my mentor and advisor, Dr. Swaminathan. I romped home with confidence and success in my practice. Choosing the right time to detach the umbilical cord from my mentor, Dr. Swaminathan, helped me gain clarity and confidence.

The same principle is also applied while dealing with our children in the broader sense. The right time to let them go on their own is an essential factor in shaping them.

Such severing of the umbilical cord is also required while bringing up children. We should severe their dependency at the right time to make them understand their problems find solutions on their own. Our help in protecting them from the government, school, and society would harm them in the long run, affecting their objective growth. Actually what is required is stepping back gradually so that they can step up and rise to the occasion to meet the challenges of life without any difficulty.

Bestowing abundant power and absolute roles to them shapes them as potential citizens of the country. Once the children grow into adults, we may feel guilty and worried when they face problems in their day to day life. Instead of stepping in to solve their issues, if we teach them and allow them to find their own solutions, it would really prepare them for practical life, making them understand their inner potential. Such practices allow them to find their own remedies. It would do a world of good for both the children and the parents.

Once, a father, Mr. Avinash, complained about his son, Abhishek, who was not at all interested in taking up any jobs. Going deeper in the conversation as a consultant, I found out that Mr. Avinash was the reason for his son's disinterest in being employed. Getting the son the costliest mobile, providing him with limitless money for his expenses and showing him a luxurious life without any strain had made the son become lethargic and disinterested in any hard work. As money was given in abundance, earning was not a motivation. If the father had run through the process of the necessity of employment, Abhishek would have proceeded in the right direction.

Parents should not become lifetime saviors for their children, indirectly draining their potential. To make the children know about life, parents need to practically educate, direct them, and allow them to perform at the appropriate time.

Emotional support is what is needed for children to move ahead in life and not the practical pushing of them in each and every instance.

In some conservative cultures, the concepts of boundaries do not exist at all. Although it is culture related issue. The impact is the same as every other case.

The experience of working with remote villagers is a great evolution by itself. A woman, Eswari, explained how she suffered after her marriage. Just within two months of her marriage, when she was getting her monthly periods, her mother-in-law, Gowri, felt bad. Gowri was keeping a very unhappy face as Eswari has not entered the level of conceiving a kid. Gowri abused Eswari for being infertile. In the subsequent months, things became worse and worse for Eswari as all Gowri's relatives started questioning her about the issue. And after the third or fourth month, people practically forced her to go for an immediate medical check-up.

Due to this perpetual questioning of all the people around, week after week, the stress on Eswari piled up. She could not concentrate on anything. She desperately had to undergo sex with her husband, Babu, just to conceive. Her anger and outbursts overtook the feeling of love. As all the efforts and therapy were in vain, Eswari categorically forced husband for a change of place. Even in therapy, she decided to go out of the current location to some other place as her emotions developed into displeasure at everybody and at herself.

This is a typical case of the invasion into the private space of others. Here entering into the psycho-emotional space of others leads to a lot of interpersonal pressure.

Another villager, a girl, Pavithra is aged 27, but she is yet to get married. To avoid unnecessary questions from other people who know her, she practically stopped talking to people, and she avoided social gatherings of any sort. She is apparently fed up of the daunting question, "Why has her marriage not happened even after so many years?" This started occupying a bigger space in her mind, and the result is that she is not able to concentrate on anything whatsoever.

People really might not mean to hurt anybody through such questions. Their intention is to initiate a conversation. But the concerned person gets affected and offended, always making the concerned to wonder why they are asked such questions.

Separateness and Togetherness – The Distinguishing Factor

"To know when to go away and when to come closer is the key to lasting relationships."

– Domenico Cleriestradac

Isolation and togetherness are two contrasting needs, but both of them are considered integral parts of relationships. The most satisfying relationship is the relationship between people who have allotted space in their togetherness. A healthy balance between the two paradoxical psychological requirements is what is very essential in a relationship. And more so in an intimate and close relationship. The differentiation of separateness is an indispensable process which helps people to be connected without being consumed by each other. Love is not just binding people; it involves respecting individuality and assisting others in the relationship to attain their greatest desires as individuals.

Even in a very close relationship, there needs to be a room for individuation and personal growth. For the relationship to be alive, it requires to breathe, for which it needs space. A relationship should be a place where people share the experience of helping the other become more than if the relationship was not there. A relationship should never be a prison or a trap.

A research, SKOWRON, has revealed that couples who demonstrate a high level of differentiation are more likely to be mutually satisfied in their relationship. Many times, we hold on tight due to the fear of losing the other person. Just because of the tightness, the other person begins to feel claustrophobic, and the probability is that he wants to break open when the hold is high.

Kannan and Arthi were deeply in love. They spent considerable time together. Arthi's possessiveness and protection gave Kannan the total sense of belongingness. The happiness was short lived as the demand went up to the stage that Arthi was expecting Kannan to talk to only her. And she required more authentication from Kannan for establishing their love.

As Kannan was not able to cope up with the anticipated demand, suffocation started setting in. There was no breathing space in the relationship. She practically had her wrist cut as Kannan was not attending to her phone call. Arthi was picking a fight with Kannan when Kannan spoke to somebody who was disliked by Arthi. At the same time, Kannan became more claustrophobic and desperately wanted to get out of the relationship with Arthi. Kannan ultimately decided that marrying Arthi would make him collapse as she was expecting him to offer more than what he can offer.

Any person, no matter how beloved, can become an irritating source of conflict if there is no personal space when there is a desire to have space. No relationship can survive an overabundance of closeness.

There is no greater way of expressing love in a relationship than by allowing the person to be himself. When the relationship is free and accepting, both the parties have little to fear.

Dependency may appear like love, but it is not. It thwarts the growth of the individual in the relationship. It seeks to receive rather than give. It works to trap rather than to liberate the other in the relationship.

Parents feel happy when children depend on them for every decision and obey them without question. Parents believe it is discipline, but in fact, it is diminishing their inherent potentiality.

In a close relationship, expecting the other person to obey you is diminishing him. Expecting the spouse to detach from others is diminishing him, expecting the other person to enmesh is diminishing him. It retards the growth of the individual in the relationship. A healthy relationship is one where the separateness is understood and respected. This would only make life interesting.

Two people, when getting married, expect each other to amalgamate and synchronize their likes, dislikes, persona, interests, and socialization. They begin to feel guilty when they tend to enjoy something individually without the other partner. Fun without the spouse would become annoying due to the guilt factor. Very often, the couple says to each other that they can't live without the other. This feeling is not the ideal feeling or it is not so great in reality. Such statements do not enunciate feelings of self-security. But on the contrast, it projects a feeling of fear to face the world alone. "I cannot live without you," cannot be taken as a statement of perfection. The right statement is, "I can live without you. But I chose to be with you, and I am always willing to be with you." It's the most practical life science statement.

It is a common scenario in many cultures, that after the marriage, the women are advised to refrain from studies, jobs, or any other desires, and have to concentrate on the married life. She would have felt some passionate thing would add great value to her character. But she would be deprived of that due to the marriage. Vice versa, the men are also advised to cut down time with their friends after the marriage. They are practically forced to forget having fun and even their own family to satisfy the better half. This is the process of seeking evidence for their love by narrowing their territory of whims and fancies. Instead of practicing their routine formulas, if couples can resort to helping each other in achieving their ambition and work towards whims and fancies of partners, it would certainly shape their married lives better.

A relationship should not become a prison

In a RELATIONSHIP which is healthy, there is a definite breathing room. There are other friends, and there are other interests, other thoughts, and other feelings. There is always a psychological space which is safely enhancing trust on each other, by giving value to the other person's interest and desires. It prevents apathy to set into the relationship.

A relationship should not be converted into a prison by our actions. A relationship should not restrict the desire to grow. On the other hand, an ideal relationship would give a sense of freedom for the people within the relationship. Here, trust is not imposed, but it comes automatically.

Even in a marriage, the couple needs to think there are some other goals for the partner to aspire and achieve. Even if one is not able to directly enter the fray and catalyze the activity of that particular sector, it is enough that he just allow his partner to have their own modus operandi to give shape to their desires.

Spiritual growth gets hampered when one partner in a relationship, in the name of tradition, undermines the other from reaching his potential. This means that you must do what I want you to do, be the person I want you to be. Your purpose in life should be what I decide to be.

Parents, consciously or unconsciously, cherish and reward the dependency of the child with them. This dependency continues when children become adults also. Parents invariably see their children as their own extension. And such a perception hides the individuality as the parents fail to see or analyze the child's character and interests, which would shape their personality. In reality, if the parents strive for the children's cause of creating their own identity, it would really augur well in the broader sense of it.

Genuine love for children should reflect in the preferred growth which would really establish individuality in them. It is definitely the role of parents to start the process of creating individuality in children.

Adolescents always feel that their parents do not bother about their likes and dislikes, and interests and disinterests. They categorically determine that the parents are only bothered about how these children appear to others in their life. As the child grows, it realizes, it is a separate entity, and it vividly shows a very transparent individuality. Practically, life demands much of a concrete contribution from the parents in the form of cultivating a mature relationship with the children with perfect boundaries.

When such an act is not executed, the feeling of incompetence and low esteem sets in. Letting their children go on their own is struggle for most parents. As the child grows, it is imperative that the parents bestow decisive powers and the right responsibilities. The parents should create situations for the children to take their own decisions. The idea should be to see the children to be molded into an autonomous personality, rather than manipulating them to cling on to them for a lifetime.

When you are letting children go or releasing them on their own route to achieve their own destination, it does not mean the parents are abandoning the children. It actually means they are experimenting with their powers in a very secure environment under proper parentship and guidance. It is a sort of detached attachment. Obviously, the children would feel they are only performing, and they also know, they have the vital backup of essential guidance from parents. This factor erases the fear in the mind of children, and they go ahead with confidence. Detached attachment gives confidence to both parents and children. While children are glad to have a buffer in the form of critical guidance, parents feel, that the children are improving their ideas in a workable manner.

I have been discussing the significance of having space leading to continuing freshness in relationship.

It is commonly seen that post-retirement, there are a lot of conflicts over petty issues. Sometimes being together all the time can lead to a deadly silence with nothing left to share. Studies have shown that being available to each other all the times leads to dryness in the relationship. Small breaks create bonding in the relationship after retirement.

A woman may feel claustrophobic as there is a complete lack of separateness. She may feel her domain is being encroached on day to day issues. A few hours of absence may make their heart fonder and add quality to their communication.

Here, I would like to discuss an activity called a *parallel play.* We have come across children in their preschool years playing with their toys in adjustment to another child. In between, he looks at what the other child is playing and shows interest. This model, when applied to couples, especially after retirement, shows that they will be less tied to each other and more interested in parallel play. Parallel play in the partnership does not suggest emotional disconnection from each other but the negotiation of autonomy and connection with each other. It demonstrates having your own interests and also being appreciative of your spouse's interest.

The need for autonomy needs to be understood and negotiated effectively as many partners may experience partners leaving to do their own thing as abandonment.

Learning from the animal's way

Animal cubs are good examples of this model. As offspring, cubs begin to function on their own as a separate entity under the safe guidance of the parent animal. The process becomes workable as the parent animal show them first and the cubs watch them fetching food for them.

Convinced that the cub has learned the art of fetching food, the parent animal releases them systematically to be on their own. Nature and wildlife offer so many examples to us for us to shape our lives in a lovely manner. Nature promotes separateness or rather individuality at some point of time. The psychological umbilical cord has to be severed from the parent at an appropriate time

During counseling, when I tell the client that the significant other needs to be given space, it is sometimes taken personally. They feel rejected and hurt. They see this desire for space as breaking away or a threat and desertion. Letting go is an integral part of relationship, and only if that is done, the actual growth starts within the relationship.

In my decades of practice, I have come across cases, where fathers used to sleep with his adolescent son, fearing that, left alone, he may fantasize about sex and may further get involved in solitary sex. Similarly, parents won't allow adolescent daughters to meet friends very often by cutting their socializing. They practically fear girls may pick up unwanted male contacts, which may cause big trouble at a later stage. It is a fallacy we believe, that when children always cling onto parents, it is only an evolution of love.

Honestly analyzing, children do not grow with their fullest abilities and fullest potential if their parents are monitoring them on a day to day basis. It is a clear submission from experts, the life skills of children are depleted when parents work as watch and ward personnel for them. This watch and ward philosophy curtails the objective growth of children in many ways.

The supervision of parents create fear in the children, and they do not come out with their individuality. If that factor of individuality is thwarted, children become diminished in the long run.

A child, Mithun, was brought for counseling by his parents, Krishna and Nutan. First, it seemed like the child was mentally retarded. But after detailed observation and study, I assessed Mithun, and he was quite normal for his age. I also found out that the parents were always fearful and overly protective of Mithun. He was not allowed to play with children of his age group. Mithun was not even allowed to go cycling as Krishna and Nutan were afraid he would get hurt.

Even for basic routines like bathing, eating, and dressing, his parents were rushing towards him to assist him. When Krishna and Nutan spoke to me, they complained that, at Mithun's age, other children functioned freely in a self-sufficient manner. They also asked how when all other children were functioning independently, how come Mithun was lacking and lagging behind. Don't you think it is a clear paradox? Everybody knows that they have not allowed Mithun to do anything on his own.

They have not exposed him to age-appropriate activities. Neither had they allowed him to take any responsibilities and face frustrations. Since the decision making is not allowed to develop, children like Mithun undergo a very difficult time, even as an adult, when they have to face situations requiring timely decision making. Even small responsibilities are sufficient to burden them. If you do not allow someone to enter the water, how he can be a master of swimming? This is a classic case of the umbilical cord not being severed at the right time.

In this case study, you should have found where the lacuna is. The jinx is only with the parents, Nutan and Krishna, who have been just petting and pampering Mithun for each and everything. Even after days of counseling for all three, they said they would allow Mithun to enter the water only after he learns swimming fully. You cannot be a kangaroo, always carrying your cub in your stomach bag. If you are going to carry it like that, how can the cub learn walking or jumping or rather how would he know about the earth?

Raji is the only child of Raghu and Ragini. As Raghu died when Raji was two years old, the total burden of bringing up Raji fell on the shoulders of

Ragini. As a single parent, Ragini toiled very hard, and sacrificed her life totally for the sake of Raji. Though she found it tough to make both ends meet, she somehow managed life and brought up Raji. Once Raji reached marriage age, she got married to Venkat, a bridegroom who was living in the same city. The idea for Ragini was clear; she searched for a bridegroom within her city as she wanted Raji to be near her for a lifetime. Every day, Ragini prepared food and sent it to Raji. Correspondingly, Raji was responding very well in the relationship to satisfy Ragini.

Mutually, Raji and Ragini were making telephone calls every hour and visiting each other every day at least once. If this system of food exchanges, phone calls, or visits were missed on even a single day, Ragini would be collapse become dejected. Raji also felt dejected on the event of some disturbances in the schedule. But this was causing a lot of mental problems for Venkat, Raji's husband, as she was concentrating more on satisfying Ragini.

Venkat got a transfer to a different city, and Raji had to go with Venkat, causing restlessness and sleeplessness to Ragini. She was severely struck by the absence of Raji in her routine. She pleaded with Raji to come back. Raji felt terribly disturbed, unable to console Ragini or convince Venkat to return.

Neither Raji nor Ragini were able to concentrate on anything, and both of them went into a state of terrible depression. Due to this family tension,

Venkat's schedule was **disturbed** and erratic. The relationship between the three got terribly disturbed and distorted, and the growth of the family was obstructed beyond limits. Here, the daughter, Raji, has failed to differentiate as she grew and continued to be enmeshed with Ragini. This failure to differentiate made the relationship go for a toss. This not only caused emotional cut-off from the mother but also between Raji and her husband.

Pleasing Others Pushes up the Pressure

To Please is a Disease

The FACTOR of unhappiness in interpersonal relationships arise mainly from our belief, which commands us to please others. Trying to please everyone around us always keeps us under pressure, seeking the approval of the so-called near and dear constantly drives us to the brink of acute tension. The phenomenon makes us lose our individuality, and our main focus moves us towards satisfying others.

Our originality immerses deep in our heart as we execute everything as per the desire of others. This originates from our childhood as our main goal is to get appreciation from parents, teachers, friends, and elders, who reward us whenever we execute things close to their heart. All our behaviors are validated by parents, and we are certified for being good, obedient, disciplined, and wiser. The real problem occurs when we start losing ourselves to these remarks. When this occurs, we categorically become an observer of our own life, forgetting the greatness of it and enjoying it. As we take care of our lives, through others' eyes, we fail to experience our excellent life.

Artificiality is not comfortable

It is the fear of rejection which prevents us from being ourselves and makes us behave like a totally different personality which craves to seek the endorsement of others.

Individuality is the quality or character of a particular person or thing that distinguishes them from others of the same kind, especially when strongly marked. "No one should part with their individuality and become that of another," is a popular quote.

Here, I would like to discuss a client, Dr. Hari, who came for a consultation and his case is peculiar. He has lost all his hair, and when a marriage proposal came, he desperately resorted to therapies and treatments, in vain.

As he was really keen on his marriage, he wore a wig when he visited to see the bride. Once the alliance was fixed, he decided to continue using the wig without revealing the actual fact. The marriage was over, and he was wearing his wig right throughout. And during the first night when the bride saw him without a wig, she was shocked and taken aback.

Honestly what shook the bride was not the hairlessness but the fake self Hari had projected to deceive her. Dr. Hari and her were not able to live a compatible life. This issue came up often, and it became a perpetual war story in their life. Something more important than hair, their trust was shaken. At the same time, an enormous effort was taken to retain this false self had deprived him of the pleasure of waiting for a novel relationship.

A lady in mid-thirties, Sowmya, was expressing her unhappiness. When she was young, she was fully taking care of her own family. Sowmya firmly believed and presumed she liked it. She pushed herself into the backseat, sacrificing a lot and giving priority to the happiness of others.

There were situations when her mother Sumithra needed her. She could not make herself available, not because she was not allowed to, but because of her own belief that her in-laws could not manage without her.

Sowmya's grief was that she could not contribute during the last days of her mother Sumithra's life. She was totally guilty of not performing what her mother wanted. She was totally in a depression due to this. She could not even express this to anybody, including her husband, Suresh. But the turning point came to her in form of her co-sister, Rashmi, who got married to her brother-in-law, Raghu.

The scenario totally changed. Even Rashmi was also committed to her mother, Madhuri, and her family. She was also contributing to her family and her relatives. But the main factor is she wanted to strike a balance between her home and, her husband, Raghu's home. Rashmi was appreciated by all in both the families. Neither Rashmi nor any of the other family members had any difficulty with the comfortable stand of Rashmi, and she actually become the first choice for everybody in the family. As Rashmi was able to say 'no' to some work, when she did not have time and accepted the assignment when she had the time, people understood her in a clear manner. And there was no problem whatsoever in her swift movement in the family.

Rashmi was the leading cause of a lot of displeasure to Sowmya. Unhappiness drove her to a lot of discomfort, and she felt everyone was considering her a doormat. In the above case study, Sowmya believed that if she was not going out of the way pleasing everyone, she would be rejected and she was not be able to take the rejection. This fear of being accepted and appreciated made her a slave. This slavery was very much self-inflicted. If she was her own self like how Rashmi was, people in the family would have taken some time to adapt but would have accepted her original self. It is only she who had scripted her married life into unhappiness, and nobody else could be blamed.

While Sowmya designed her life as a doormat, no other person could help her. When you air a feeling that you *don't count*, that spreads in the environment and becomes a virtual reality. We should have our own individuality to avoid this predicament and self-assassination of our own character.

Suppressing our individuality and losing our own identity makes us suffer and we only explore the reasons for people liking or disliking us. Most of the time, the freedom to be yourself or not yourself is your own creation and not others.

Understand who you are first and analyze your own limitations, assert your positive and negative factors, know to handle your own personality in the fittest way possible, and let the world accept you as a straightforward, frank, and transparent personality. We attach a lot of blinkers to our heads, which affects our free moments. In the above case study, the contradictory characters of Sowmya and Rashmi clearly describe this.

Sowmya was always at displeasure, unable to serve the mother, Sumithra. Rashmi was also taking care of her own family. She was able to balance the bar, by properly analyzing and asserting her own role.

Since Rashmi was nourishing herself properly and was also in a position to contribute to her husband, Raghu's home, she earned respect from all corners and commanded great respect from all. All pegs were falling in right squares for her, and the secret was she was able to command and control her own personality to get the desired results.

Rashmi made herself count her everywhere. "**I do count,**" became a frank truth of her after marriage. While Sowmya was airing the feeling, "I don't count." The people around her echoed the same, and that became a reality, and as described by herself, she adorned the role of a doormat. It is called carving one's own destiny. The paradox is that although people enjoy benefitting from one who is passive, the fact is that no one admires and respect a person who allows themselves to be enslaved.

This means that a woman who dominated her husband although may enjoy the privilege but may not be able to count on him for making major decisions regarding their family and children. An adolescent who is able to get his way by rebelling to his passive father ultimately may not respect his father or look upon him as a source of strength.

One thing which keeps us from expressing our needs is that we will be labeled as selfish. The fact is that nobody knows your real needs and necessities than your own self. Who can better know what you require than yourself?

The payoff you get is double when you are able to be your own self. One is you get to be yourself, and it saves a lot of effort to pretend and please others. The other is that people around you start understanding and respecting you for your uniqueness over a period of time. Being true to oneself is very significant for self-harmony and for harmony in a relationship. One needs to listen to one's feelings, to trust one's heart, and be authentic to oneself. Ask yourself to let go of being nice and pleasing others so that you can be the real you and people see the real you. When you are true to yourself, you cannot betray anyone else. Milton Avery rightly points out, "To be able to be oneself and not have to disown one's value to please another, that is what love is all about."

Carving individuality occupies so much prominence in one as that only decides and determines a blossoming future for us. Never can you offer a cup of tea to somebody if your own cup is empty.

Similarly when you are searching for happiness, how you can bestow happiness to others? Throughout our lives, we add to our own burdens for the causes of others. We feel others are fragile and they cannot be hurt. Hence to have a smooth relationship with them, we hurt our own self day in and day out.

Sketching our own identity and individuality should be offered a very prominent position in our agenda as if we do not act in proper time designing the same, we may go enslaved. "YES," "Sure," "I will," and "I will give," comes out naturally from our mouth many times as we practically push ourselves to do things fearing being labeled uncompassionate.

"No," "I can't," "I will think about it," and "Give me some time," may sound rude and erratic. But in reality, these are good protective devices, which protect us from being manipulated. Here you do not make commitments in haste but give yourself the freedom and time to think. To commit under the pressure of pleasing and winning their appreciations is not a good idea for a healthy relationship as it creates a lot of bitterness in the long run.

Dysfunctional belief – sacrifice

One of the common dysfunctional beliefs carried generation after generation is that, in a relationship, one has to sacrifice one's desire and happiness for others. Unhealthy sacrifice is often perpetuated by an enormous fear that your happiness is selfish. This is a dysfunctional idea which collapses us in our lives. Sacrifices lead to self-denial and bitterness in life. Such sacrifices cannot be a healthy foundation for a good relationship or a happy life. It is only a sheer paradox. How can you be happy by giving others what is cherished and loved by you? When you yield to others sometimes or the other, you hold another person responsible for the pain that comes with giving something away. It creates a covert expectation to receive. When this receiving has not happened, it gives a feeling of having given too much to the relationship.

If the individual chooses to part with something just for the pleasure of giving, it does not cause pain. A lady when asked by her family to sacrifice her job for the sake of her child may later regret doing so. Here, the lady makes the decision to leave the job in order to prevent herself from guilt and underneath this guilt was the belief that one has to sacrifice oneself when it comes to significant others, and if she does not sacrifice, she is not a responsible mother. Although unconsciously, she has made the decision under both internal and external pressure. This pressure may show up in her relationship with her child and others.

In the long run, if you ask how many people to whom you sacrificed are really grateful to you, you may know that people never realized it was a sacrifice. They thought that you wanted to do what you have done. In another situation, the lady herself chooses to leave the job to enjoy being with the child. Here, her acceptance of the decision leads to satisfaction and she will be in harmony with herself and others. Owning the decision gives confidence and mental energies to face the consequences which come with the decisions.

During therapy, I came across an engineering college professor, Mr. Suriya Narayan, and his wife, Mrs. Nagarathinam, who are living together under one roof without any regular interaction, whatsoever. Actually the professor was in love with another girl by the name of Padma, right from his student days.

Not knowing this, his parents were planning for his marriage to Nagarathinam. The entire family felt happy about their marriage. The confidence of the elders grew more and more, as Suriya Narayan didn't raise any objection.

Perceiving that the bond between both the families would become powerful, in the event of marriage between Surya Narayan and Nagarathinam, the arrangements were accelerated, and the marriage happened. Professor Surya Narayan never revealed the truth that he is in love with some other girl and he was not at all convinced of getting married to Nagarathinam.

Surya Narayan felt reluctant to utter even a single word on his love affair as he felt that it may affect his parents, Ganapathy and Kalavathy. Also, he felt for Nagarathinam, who was totally innocent. He strongly believed his refusal to marry her would definitely affect Nagarathinam's life. Added to that, his stern decision, to refuse the marriage with Nagarathinam would affect the bond between both the families.

He clearly felt all concerned would suffer a shock if he revealed his love affair. Due to this dilemma, without any love, affection, passion interest, or attraction, Surya Narayan, got married to Nagarathinam. The marriage happened, and after that, it was only robotic movements in the daily routine. He could never have any romantic interactions with Nagarathinam.

His mind was totally occupied with thoughts of his lover, Padma, and these thoughts made him feel much more imprisoned in his marriage. Surya Narayan, after the marriage, felt he had done a gross injustice to his lover, Padma, causing much more worries for him. He was not going home early, after the college hours, as he felt going home was a punishment. He feared holidays as he had to be at home without even talking to his wife, Nagarathinam.

Nagarathinam was crying within herself as she was not able to let anybody including her parents know about this. It would collapse their family completely as she was the only daughter of her parents.

Months passed by, a family meeting happened, as both parents felt there was something wrong with the married life of Surya Narayan and Nagarathinam. And after persistent pressure, Suryanarayana revealed the truth about his love affair with Padma. Though both his parents and in-laws were taken aback by the fact, they felt they should accept the reality, getting an uncontrollable jolt.

Nagarathinam was also keeping her fingers crossed about what would be her future. They all felt the professor should have asserted himself and revealed the love affair before the marriage. Everybody was very unhappy with his passivity.

At this point, everybody said, "We could have got you married as per your wishes if you had discussed this earlier and were clear about it." His lover Padma also got married in the meantime and got settled in a different life altogether.

Surya Narayan analyzed the consequences in his mind. If he voiced out his feelings, he would be disowned by his family, his father would die because of stress, and their ties with the uncle's family would break. He felt it will be too selfish on his part to cause so much damage.

Ultimately what happened was much more than what he feared. It was likely that if he was very clear about his decision and his life, his family would have accepted this over a period of time. Thinking that he should not displease anybody in the family, Surya Narayan was hiding the truth, and the result was actually that he had displeased all the people around him with his attitude.

Thinking that he had sacrificed for the family, he has virtually and practically killed the ambiance and the harmony of the family. In the entire process, not even one person was happy in the family.

There was a similar case of Naresh. Although he had a very lucrative job, he was not able to give himself and his family luxury, comfort, or a vacation. His is a huge extended family, and somebody or the other expects him to help physically and financially. He strongly believed it was not okay to say no and he kept letting go of his own mental peace.

Now when he expects his relatives to reciprocate, it causes great pain when they do not do that. Sacrifice has an element of expectation, and when those are not met, it causes a lot of regret. He recalls the time when he canceled the planned trip with his family because his presence was required by one of the relatives.

To believe that you have a choice

Many times, we feel others may not approve our likes and dislikes. Of course, it is true. We have been constantly trained to succumb to manipulative behavior. We always have think once we commit to something, even by force, for somebody's sake, to satisfy them, there is no choice for us to revert back. But the fact is we do always have abundant choices, either before taking a decision or even after that, before the actual performance of the act.

Everybody has the right to change their own decision at any point of time. The availability of choices are always in your mind, and the steadfast ability to go by the gut feeling will always make you a stronger and sturdy personality. People may make demands from you. But it is absolutely on you whether to agree or disagree, or to how much quantum you can agree.

James was in love with Juliet and James felt insecure whenever Juliet went out with any other person or when she is on a second call, neglecting his call. Due to the desperation for her not attending to him or not giving priority to him, he went to the level of consuming poison. His mother, Mariam, pleaded with the girl to continue the relationship. Although Juliet had decided to marry James, she now decided to change her decision and take a back step

She realized that to continue the relationship with James would require a lot of effort and there were only remote possibilities of having a harmonious relationship in the long run. On the contrary, I have come across people who very well realized that the decision was not correct but still continued due to fear of opening up to others. Letting go of the fear that your happiness is selfish creates new possibilities of growth and joy.

Gender-based belief – An obstacle

Another common belief centers around gender, which prevents one from being oneself. The role of the female is always that of supporting the male, and the role of the male is that of the breadwinner of the family. The ideal way would have been to strike a balance between the two roles, first to live her own life and the second to support her male counterpart in the family. Quite often, she feels tremendous guilt when she is thinking of her own life. The woman feels it is not correct that they opt for giving priority to their hobby, passion, and interests. Hence, thinking that any step to satisfy her ambition may risk her relationship becomes the contention of the women.

Man tends to believe that because of his gender, he has to adorn the role of the breadwinner of the family. Due to this vital role and his commitment to the family, he is deprived of many of his passions, interests, desires, and ambitions. Nobody nurtures or even bother about his whims and fancies.

A factory worker, Mujahid, got married to Salma. And he came for a consultation, after the marriage, unable to strike a balance between being on his own and being a husband after the marriage. Before marriage, Mujahid used to play cricket on the weekends. That was enjoyable for him. He strongly felt his weekend game of cricket, recharged him for the forthcoming week. After the marriage, he was deprived of this weekend enjoyment and pleasure.

This indirect denial or refraining from the game made him unhappy and pushed him to a monotonous life.

Seema and Tharak got married after much opposition from Tharak's family. Seema made up her mind to win the hearts of everyone in his family. Starting from the first day, she began taking all the responsibility for the household. She gave up completely on her passions, and on her friends.

Days passed by. By not being her own self, Seema was drained of energy day in and day out. The false mask of Seema suffocated her to the core. And this was glaringly reflected in the strains in the relationship. Seema invariably felt she was doing so much for Tharak's family. She quarreled with him, citing that she was practically sacrificing her life for Tharak's family. Seema pertinently angled her anger on Tharak. The revolt gradually started, and Seema took the opportunity to go to her mother's place whenever time permitted.

Whenever she visited her mother, Mahima, she was her own self in the right comfort zone. She dwelled on those days with total relief. Perpetual travel to Mahima's place caused a lot of worries to Tharak, and he was starting quarrels with Seema, time and again. Due to this, the frequent visits of Seema to her mother's place increased. This shows that putting your small desires of day to day life in the back seat accumulates pain and it shows itself in the relationship. The truth is that you cannot sacrifice yourself and have a happy relationship. The activities which Seema and Tharak were enjoying before marriage were recharging elements and letting them go under the pretext of stereotype belief caused them stress.

This is due **to** the total submission of the artificial face of Seema to Tharak's family. Because Seema was yielding to them, they anticipated more and more from her. Instead of that, right from the beginning, if Seema had behaved closer to her real self, things would have been different.

When we perform things of our choice, we would less likely be confronted with the issues we may not like. Whereas when we have to heed to the desires and idea of others, we would be definitely burdened by the things which would be expected from us. Working by conscious choice would be accepted and received well by oneself. Initially, it may be tough for anybody to accept the originality of anybody as everybody had to live their own lives before contributing to others. But as the time passes by, the others around would understand it is not easy to take anybody for granted for their individual benefits

When you say YES to another, make sure you don't say NO to yourself.

Enmeshment in the Relationship

Ram is a physician and belongs to a very conservative and close-knit family. His father passed away when he was in high school and from then his elder brother, who was fifteen years older to him, took responsibility. All the major decisions were made by him. Ram and everybody else in the family had a high regard for his brother for the way he took all the responsibly. There were times when his elder brother had to forgo his happiness for the sake of the family. After Ram completed his studies, the family as a whole decided to get him married to a doctor.

He got married to Gayathri, who was also a physician and had a private practice. After marriage, Ram's brother was not okay with the idea of Gayathri seeing male patients, and he conveyed his displeasure to Ram expecting him to intervene. Although Ram believes that it is not ethical to do that, since he had a high regard for the brother, he could not displease him.

This caused a lot of rifts between Gayathri and Ram.

In this family, the power flow was vertical. Although Ram felt claustrophobic, he could not communicate his feelings to his brother. The predominant emotion of Ram, in this case, was the guilt of displeasing the brother. In such families, fusing with one another passes from one generation to another and people within this system do not feel there is anything wrong in it although they may feel emotionally cut-off.

From the outside, it may look like love, respect, and obedience, but a lot of oppression is felt by individuals within the setup.

Ideally, children are launched into their adult lives from their families, prepared to think for themselves and with a well-developed efficacy and identity of their own. However, when families are tightly wound, this doesn't always happen. When children are raised to conform to their parents' expectations of who they are, what they believe, and how they think and feel, that individuation which is so necessary to being truly independent doesn't occur. Healthy families allow for differences in their members; adults and children alike. Growing up is a process of exploration, and healthy families allow for a child to develop according to their own individual and unique characteristics.

Children are not told how they should feel or think, but are encouraged to make up their own minds and express what they are feeling without being judged. As children grow older, enmeshed families can hit heavy walls of conflict when the natural, healthy questioning of adolescents challenges parents with 'too rigid' expectations for their children's behavior.

Teenagers can differ from their parents, and they often need a few years of wide variance from their parents before they settle into what feels right to them. That's a healthy process. There is mental, emotional, and overall psychological difference between people, and to understand and appreciate this difference, leads to growth. To have a point of view which is different from others is healthy. Families that are enmeshed often have a set of spoken or unspoken rules that govern the members' behaviors even into adulthood. There is a strong belief that *sameness is oneness*.

What the family feels and expect from you is what is right. Never mind that you are 45 years old and have been on your own for 27 years. The cost of being different is to be cut off.

Even as adults, you will conform to the wishes of 'the family' instead of making your own mind up about very crucial issues. Enmeshed families considered as rigid systems become locked-in over time, and these roles and patterns can be very hard to break out of unless the family as a whole understands that this enmeshment is unhealthy and wishes to change.

If you are dealing with trying to make healthy choices for your own life and experiencing the fall-out of being 'different' in an enmeshed family, you undergo a lot of tug of war. It is a herculean task to dare to do things differently. But the fact is that, over a period of time, people will start accepting you thinking that this is how you are.

If you are in an enmeshed family and you have a need or desire for a life that isn't in compliance with the family, you need to actively do it rather than expecting people to mind read.

The eminent psychologist, Seligman, conducted an experiment utilizing dogs as a specimen. He placed one dog in a box where there was a provision for escaping. The second dog was placed in another box, where there was no provision for getting out. Both the dogs were initially given periodical shocks, and both of them tried to move out from the box. The first dog succeeded as there was an escape route. And the second could not as there was no way and it was totally blocked.

After some time, the second dog which was not able to escape from the box due to no availability of an exit was placed in the first box, where there was an outlet for escaping. But, thinking that there won't be any way out, the second dog never even tried to escape, despite persistent shocks. So to say, it never even had the initiative to escape, thinking that it is its fate to get blocked up there. This state of mind Seligman calls *learned helplessness*.

Seligman's theory can be very well extended to human behavior. A child is given no decision making power, at least until its school days. In case, as an exception, a child takes a decision, it is imperative that there would be some criticism or punishment awaiting it. Due to this fact, even when the child becomes an adult, he feels he does not have the freedom to take any decisions. Frozen in helplessness, he allows others to encroach into his freedom and decision making and allows the stealing of his valuable rights. Thus the situation puts him in a cage, where there is no chance of escape, but to depend on others for any decision.

Autonomy is usually considered as the main principle in making decisions about individuals. Children and particularly adolescents have the capacity to take part in decision making

In a parent-child relationship, the over-involvement of the parents in children's life becomes a cause for concern. It practically becomes an encroachment into the children's choicest territory, and it scans the tiny details, of children's outfit. This is described as *enmeshment*. Such enmeshed relationships are very unhealthy. In the above example, we see dogs becoming helpless and giving up on trying to bring about change. Similar experiments were conducted with human beings by Seligman, and it demonstrates that humans were susceptible to giving up all hope when put in an environment where the negative outcome was beyond their control.

If we put an individual in an environment where bad things happen to them, and they have no control over them to stop them, depression and disengagement will eventually follow. It can happen in an abusive and a negative work environment, and it can happen in an abusive relationship too. I have come across relationships where one of the spouses is abusive, and the other tries their best to combat the abuse in various possible ways. But as times goes by, the sense of a lack of control over the abuse sets in, and it leads to complete freezing. I have come across some cases where even if the realization happens and the abusive partner and is willing to change, the victim has entered into a stage of learned helplessness where the mind has given up on any hope.

Enmeshment is highly dysfunctional

Enmeshment proves to be highly dysfunctional as the emotional boundaries are unclear. People are not allowed to function independently. The enmeshment or fusing can happen between parent and a child, adult couples, and sometimes to the entire family. Catching each other's emotions leads to a lack of autonomy. All concerned would have a sense of guilt when they do something for themselves. There is lot anxiety which is injected in the individuals which curtails their free movement.

The sense of individuality and originality vanishes in the fear of satisfying others, and most of the time, it gives way for mixed emotions.

A newly married bridegroom, Sekar, wants to go for an outing and wished to have a jolly evening with his spouse, Suchithra. But the mother of Sekar, Girija, always wished and expected Sekar to be with her during his leisure time.

As in the present juncture, Sekar prefers to go with his wife, Suchithra. Girija is unable to digest that she would be missing her son for that evening. Girija expresses her displeasure subtly by not eating and not moving with others comfortably. This attitude of Girija caused Sekar, to worry and he started to refrain from going out with Suchithra in the evenings as that may distress Girija. This not only diluted his relationship with his wife but also his mother.

Sekar sacrificed his own feelings and emotions to please his mother, and it mounted as anger eventually. Sekar's bond with Suchithra also got distorted as he is completely entangled with Girija. As there was no space for Suchithra, it evoked a disturbance in the relationship of the couple.

If the process of differentiation had happened when Sekar was entering adolescence, the situation wouldn't have become so critical. As it had not happened in this case, the enmeshment was intact, unable to sketch the boundaries between Girija and Sekar. Due to not fixing boundaries, the relationship had entered the problem zone. In this case, the mother herself was not aware of the chaos her behavior was causing to the couple. She believes that this is how things should be and this is what she believed in.

In the case of enmeshment, the concerned person loses his identity as he is totally attached to the other person and works towards their interests. The parent who enmeshes the child seeks to control the son or the daughter. And this practically curtails the bond which has to be formed between the couple.

Enmeshed relationship lack healthy boundaries

Enmeshed relationships are those that lack healthy psychic boundaries. We lose a sense of where we end, and another begins. Our sense of individuality is compromised. If our identity is wrapped up in meeting the other person's needs, our own life goals are thwarted. We become a stranger to our own desires, and our confidence can take a hit.

The following may be signs of enmeshment:

- ✦ An inability to control our emotional involvement with another person.
- ✦ An exaggerated sense of responsibility for the other person's feelings.
- ✦ Guilt or anxiety when not preoccupied with the other person's experience.
- ✦ Intense fear of conflict in the relationship.
- ✦ An inability to carry on if the other person is unhappy.

Enmeshment can take a physical toll on us as well. A migraine, back or neck pain, and stomach upset can all be somatic manifestations of a relationship that's too fused. Our bodies speak of a pain that our minds have yet to discover. Consider, for example, a daughter, Gopika, who doesn't understand why she feels lethargic for hours after she gets off the phone with her depressed mother, Gayathri. Gopika is identified with the mother psychic pain.

One can be enmeshed with a parent, sibling, or partner. In my practice, enmeshment shows up in a variety of relationships. There's the 40-year old man, Rakshan, who is afraid to move to another city because his father, Sethu, who lives next door, might disown him. There's the 35-year old woman, Jayashree, who can't find her own voice because she's afraid of stirring up conflict with her overanxious husband, Jagan. And there's the 50-year old woman, Bhavani, who feels responsible for her sister, Brindha's alcoholic rages.

People are not happily fused into a relationship. They feel being entangled, and their belief system does not allow them to come out of it.

If you can release yourself from a relationship that's too fused, a lot can change. Personal, as well as professional goals, can be identified and then realized.

How do you disentangle an enmeshed relationship? Just by being consciously aware of it…

Enmeshment is a corrosive bondage where one person gets pushed into other's life and seeks to do only whatever pleases that person. In this kind of relationship, the weapon of guilt always looms large, and it manipulates to threaten. The growing child develops a fear that the world is so dangerous and he can't survive in this world without his sought-after person.

Children and adults who are in an enmeshed relationship are invariably pushed to a feeling that they are selfish when they perform as per their own wishes. They obviously feel that they are responsible to make another person happy and contented. Often this is reinforced from childhood and extends to adulthood, saying that he or she is obedient, sensitive, and nice. They feel trapped by these words.

Enmeshments can also be mild as well as extreme. It depends upon how much an individual has arrived at his own individuality.

In my practice, I have come across couples who enmesh each other mutually or one enmeshing the other under the cover of protecting the spouse. She or he may feel claustrophobic as she or he may not be able to be their own selves. They may say that they may not live without the other, not even allowing the partner to meet and move with parents. The enmeshment may even thwart them from socializing. Wherever the enmeshed wants to go, the other person also wanted to accompany due to the factor of security.

A woman will get anxious when her husband gets closer to his family or friends, talking with them regularly. Due to this, the wife may prefer the husband go on business tours which would deprive him of chances of meeting his family and other close friends.

Sometimes, the parents may enmesh one of their children, citing them as their favorite child. They will provide her with all that she requires, just spanning around her in the name of love. Here, not only is this child burdened but also all the other children of the parents are alienated from the parents and the family as such. They practically lose the family bondage, which is required in the formative years for any child.

The traps which are used are the 'blame game', 'guilt', and 'being nice'. Here, the person who is enmeshed often blames others for unhappiness. There would be no sense of control for the enmeshed individual, and she practically loses her individuality.

Enmeshment – A loss of connection with the self

Nasima, 26 years old, was working as a lecturer in a private college. Her parents, Akhtar and Zarina, constantly claim her life is their life, and they cannot live without her. They periodically utter that her success is their success. Even when she is busy at the office, both Akhtar and Zarina used to call her periodically to know about her safety on an hourly basis. Added to that, each of the parents, take their own happy time in the call to grumble about their individual issues and the issues bothering the home on the whole. On all weekends, they want Nasima to be with them only, not permitting her to go to any friends' places or office trips.

The thought of the marriage practically displeased and panicked her as her parents may be deprived of her company. Nasreen clearly draws a line, and she seeks someone in the vicinity of parents. As there was practically no choice, this added to Nasima's worries as she loses herself and also the connection with herself.

She felt guilty when she was not able to call her parents frequently. She did a lot of things which she disliked for the sake of parents as she did not want to displease them through any of her actions. She really felt GUILTY about saying no to their demands. She made remarkable persistent sacrifices as she had no other go but to resort to achieve her parents' dreams for her. In the process, she practically forgot her individual desires and dreams.

It is like conducting a puppet show in your life with a person, manipulating people and situations based on their ideas and opinions.

In a parent-child relationship, the over-involvement of the parents in the children's life becomes a cause for the worry. And it practically becomes encroachment into the children's choicest territory. It scans the tiny details of a child'sq outfit. Such enmeshed relationships are very unhealthy.

Growing up is a process of exploration, and healthy families allow for a child to develop according to their own individual and unique characteristics. Children who love art are encouraged and supported even if mom doesn't value art herself. Children who love music or theatre are supported in those interests, whether the dad had football and soccer in mind or not. Children are not told how they should feel or think, but are encouraged to make up their own minds and express what they are feeling without being judged. As children grow older, enmeshed families can hit heavy walls of conflict when the natural, healthy questioning of adolescents challenges parents with 'too rigid' expectations for their children's behavior.

Teenagers need to form their own identity which differs from their parent's, and they often need a few years of wide variance from their parents before they settle into what feels right to them. That's a healthy process.

Enmeshment and the resultant suffocation

A couple, Manoj and Priya, have been married for 15 years. Both of them were running a family business. They were together all the time. Whenever Priya wanted to go out, he also accompanied her. She says there is no time when he is out of the vicinity. Manoj says he loves her so much that he cannot live a moment without her. She longs to go to her friends and relatives, and have some time for herself without him. Fearing that he will feel hurt, she never voiced out her desires. Once when she was planning a vacation with her sisters, he also accompanied her. Manoj felt rejected as he felt that she spent a lot of time talking to her sisters. This became a reason for a huge fight between the two of them and went to the extent of Priya breaking the relationship.

Here, the needs of both of them were very different. He expected her to completely get enmeshed into himself whereas she was looking for some space in the relationship. He was not able to understand that, even in a very close and loving relationship, people look for space.

This need for space differs from individual to individual. For the healthy functioning of a relationship, it is mandatory that the needs be understood, and clues need to be gathered about the other person's psychological requirements.

Rajini was married for two years. Her husband, Rajiv, is working in an IT company. He works around the week and has the weekend off. Rajini is highly fused with her family, which is her mother, father, and sister. She goes to her mother's place on Fridays and expects him to come and stay with her. He wanted to spend time with his wife and child. He wanted to eat and sleep at the time he wanted to. Over a period of time, this led to a lot of suffocation in him. He refused to go to her mother's house during weekends. The weekend she stayed with her husband, her parents made a big hue and cry. They tried injecting feelings of guilt in all possible ways. Not able to make a decision, Rajini was stuck. Her relationship with her husband got more strained day by day.

Here, Rajini's family of origin is highly enmeshed, and as she was brought up in that environment, she is not able to see the pitfall of the system. Her guilt does not allow her to break open from the system.

In such families, the marriage of children is a threat to parents. Here, a lot of disturbances among the couple arises due to the inability of the parents and others to cut-off in a healthy way. The first few years of marriage are a time when bonding has to be developed between the couple and with the extended family. In many cases, this does not develop due to the lack of space to form the relationship identity.

In the enmeshment relationship, the weaker of the two experience and carry the emotions of the other person. This can reflect in many ways. First, that the enmeshed individual may feel that the emotions are actually hers, causing her to solve the problems which are not hers. She bears the weight of her partner and absorbs their emotions as her own. In the process, the additional emotional burden and conflicts happen within herself. This can lead to health hazards and weakens the individual who is suffering in the enmeshment.

The process of enmeshment is not consciously to control the other person, but since it works in a person's favor, it is reinforced. Many times, a person, a couple, or others who are in the status of an enmeshment relationship are not aware of alternative ways of responding. Such people are deprived of their emotional time and space, or rather they do not possess any substantial relationship with anyone other than the ENMESHING person.

75-year-old, Bharani, has many grown-up children. All of them were married now and settled in their life. But Bharani was categorically enmeshed with her husband, Balaram, who practically depends on her for each and everything, right from their marriage date. He won't do the smallest of his own work, right from taking the dress for the day until wearing the shoes. Balaram was practically expecting Bharani to do all the tasks that he has to do at home. Bharani also felt it is her prime and duty to do whatever Balaram wanted.

Sometimes, Bharani wished to meet people of her age group to spend time with them and to break away from the monotony *of husband service.* She would not leave him even for a single day thinking that he will not be able to manage without her. She completely deprived herself of any liberty. She, in fact, enjoyed her husband's dependency on her. This was working in Balaram's favor, and hence he continued to be fused on to her. This led to more and more dependency on her.

She was not worried about this, but on the contrast. Bharani was feeling proud about her total service to Balaram. Feeling pride, she used to tell her sons and daughters that no one else except her would have taken care of her husband.

Despite all that commitment from Bharani to Balaram, in case, if Bharani showed the slightest gesture of tiredness or discomfort, Balaram would be furious with her. He would straight away go to the mode of eternal silence as a protest to Bharani's attitude on that day. In case of a delay when he called her, Balaram was shutting himself, and this was injecting a lot of guilt on Bharani.

This type of reaction from Balaram caused anger to Bharani at some point of time. She was not able to show anger towards Balaram, and she angled all that anger at her children in the name of blame.

Balaram bought her lot of expensive clothes and saris and expected Bharani to wear one after one as per his schedule. In the case of Bharani liking a dress and Balaram not liking it, Bharani would immediately act as per the wish of Balaram and change the dress against her own wishes just to satisfy Balaram. She was not raising even the smallest objection or displeasure about that. Bharani was more conscious about her words whenever she talked to Balaram. Bharani would not pour out her feelings to Balaram about her dislikes or non-alignment at any point of time.

Such behavior was reinforced by people in the extended family. She was struck by health issues and later it was diagnosed as an advanced stage of cancer. On knowing that she was attacked by cancer, the first thought that came to her mind was, 'I have never lived my life for myself. Now the final call of life had practically come'. She felt the heights of anger towards her husband, and she started detaching herself from Balaram. I remember the quote of Dr. Scott Peck, *"There is no worst bitterness than to reach the end of your life and realize you have not lived at all."*

All of us would have crossed this enmeshed stage, to some degree. But when it goes out of bounds, the feeling of dissatisfaction and discontent gets its way, and categorically, it makes us reject the person who enmeshed us. And we tend to feel so and so has not allowed us to live our own life, with our own likes, desires, and ambitions.

To work above enmeshment

What is essential and crucial in life is empowering yourself. Dealing with your own thoughts, expressions, and wishes makes you empowered. And it is also imperative to inform and impress on people that they are only responsible for their lives and not you.

The process of empowering starts when you start telling yourself periodically, "I have the right to go by my own thoughts, feelings, and actions and design my life as per my wishes." By cutting out the emotional blinkers, you can take command of your own life.

Once you allow and occupy your own deserved space in life to exhibit your original individuality, the relationship with all others will be much better. The parent-children relationship would become healthy and stronger when parents take responsibility for the happiness of children, and at the same time, children are allowed their space to take up the responsibility for their happiness.

It is a similar concept of oxygen mask in an airplane. If you do not wear your emotional oxygen mask first, neither will you save yourself nor would you be in a position to help anyone.

In a healthy relationship, people maintain their identity and are respected for it. Here, people trust in their ability to fix things in their own life. They choose to be with people who would respect individuality, rather than living for the needs of other people.

As an adult, having your own thinking power in a precise, perfect system and having a strong sense of decision making power is what is needed for society to respect you. Healthy bondage allows individuality and perfect connectivity.

Setting small spaces for yourself in your daily routine, create and carve healthy boundaries for you to feel safe to secure you being yourself.

Radhika left her home to join a company. Her mother, Rathnamala, expected her to call now and then and update her with the details of whatever happened right from the morning, each day. Instead of telling the Rathnamala this practice was suffocating, Radhika empathized with her mother, thinking that Rathnamala was doing all this with maximum love and care only.

Actually, Radhika should have let Rathnamala understand that she can talk to her only during a particular time of the day or week freely without affecting her daily schedules and stealing time which she had to spend in her office on her job. The failure to let her mother know the practical facts that made her enter a situation with a lot of problems.

Carry Home Message From the Chapter

The most precious gift you give yourself is the freedom to be yourself. Let go of the mask and dare to be YOU.

Healthy limits are self-protective, and NO is a protective instrument.

Pressure to please people WILL lead to unhappiness and disharmony.

The more you focus on fusing and confirming, the more you move away from yourself.

PART - 2

The Perfect Connect is the Precise Need

"You may forget with whom you laughed, but you may never forget with whom you wept."

— Kahil Gibran

The 'need to be understood' is the strongest feeling, which is sought by all. Analyzing psychologically, feeling understood makes one relate completely to others and show more transparency in their relationship. And that allows us to confess more and more of the inner world to the other.

If we do not establish the perfect 'connect', which is the essential ingredient, the objective of communication won't be achieved. Empathy is the key aspect to achieve indispensable 'connect' in relationships.

Carl Roger explains, "Empathy is entering the private perceptual world of the other person and become thoroughly at home in it. Actually, empathy amounts to mentally living the other person's life without any judgment. Making an attempt to enter the frame of the other person's reference and sends a message of respect.

Genuinely understanding the other person is the key to a healthy relationship. When one person in the relationship tries to understand the other, it's more likely he will be understood.

When a child fails in an examination, he feels disappointed, dismayed, dejected, depleted, and disgruntled. He feels humiliated in front of his peers and teachers. He gets into an area of confusion on how to explain his failure to parents. He worries how his parents would react. He enters home with heavily loaded feelings and fingers totally crossed.

Although the mother may be disappointed too, she works with the help of the connect. She puts her hand around the child's shoulder and provides an ambiance and atmosphere for the child to get into a zone of comfort. She converses with him more to make him be cool and concentrate again on what is needed to be worked on. Here, when he is understood, he feels secure to the point of working on the area he has missed.

This approach does not cause a scratch on the relationship. Here, the communication doors are open. The child himself is aware as to where he has missed. When the mother started accepting him along with his failures, he became more and more comfortable opening up to his mother. To be empathetic is to utilize a tool to achieve an alliance.

To move the conversation in the affirmative direction, it is essential that the feelings need to be allowed to ventilate. This helps open the door to work on future issues. If the mother had initiated the conversation with blame, the child would have become defensive by blaming school, teachers, and parents. He would have used striking back as a strategy to protect himself.

My experience with prisoners after they have committed brutal crimes is that when told bluntly what they have done is wrong, most of them have immediate urge to prove what they have done was the requirement of the time.

Many of our problems have to be understood to be related to. Newly married Rakesh used to get annoyed when his wife narrated whatever bitter went between her and mother-in-law. He either tried to become defensive or fought with the mother on issues shared by his wife. During counseling, he said, "Although I fight with my mother for her, she keeps saying that I do not understand her feelings." When his wife, Kalpana, was asked to reflect on this, she said, "I never wanted him to fight with his mother. I just wanted him to operate at a level and make me feel that I am understood."

Despite the son performing the perfect mediation between his mother and his wife, neither of them got convinced or satisfied. Actually, this is not what they were looking for... Instead of that, if the husband, establishes a CONNECT with his spouse, the wife would have felt that her husband has understood her.

To understand that there is a reason why a person behaved the way he did is very important.

Person-centered communication over issue-centered communication

It is imperative in such cases that we direct the communication PERSON centered than the ISSUE centered. To take care of the issue, the feelings of the concerned person to be taken care of. It is a common scenario when somebody approaches us to discuss some issue or problem, our mind automatically starts searching for suggestions and advice which we can offer to the person, to address his issue.

When we are habituated to do this, we automatically start giving ideas to the other person to work out his life. The moment we do that, the other person starts, **"Yes - but.** Yes, you are right but, you know... but." Because what may look fair in your life may not look workable for him. The ideas which you were giving is from your frame of reference and which may not be agreeable to him.

The fact here is that everybody is capable of resolving their issues, they all have the potential to do so. What will only help this person is the emotional support to talk out. As you are listening, he opens up more and more, thereby he becomes clearer and clearer.

Our mind is like a pressure cooker. Unless the steam is released, it cannot be open, and any input won't work out.

When an IT employee, Mahesh, approached me for consultation, I came across interesting observations. He was really hardworking and sincere. He was awaiting his appraisals with curiosity. On the contrary, he received disappointing ratings. When he approached his immediate boss, Jacob, he tried to justify the given ratings while pointing out flaws Mahesh had made in the work. This defensiveness from his boss prevented Mahesh from venting out his real feelings.

Jacob forcefully analyzed the tasks done by Mahesh and gave out the reasons for the ratings given for him. He summarised that the ratings and findings were only for the betterment of his career and asked to understand his drawbacks which were obstructing his growth.

While **Mahesh** was looking to be addressed at an emotional level, the boss, Mr. Jacob, was communicating at a logical level. While Mahesh was trying to express his disappointment, Jacob was not at able to understand him and vice versa. What Jacob was implying with logic was not taken in good stead by Mahesh as his mind was clouded with emotions.

Criticism serves no purpose. It is futile. It puts the person in a defensive mode, and he will tend to justify himself. When an individual is criticized, his pride and sense of self is highly wounded. The person who is criticized develops resentment towards the other person. Moreover, much more than the criticism, it is the method of attack which people really resent. Ongoing criticism in a relationship leads to the demise of a relationship. To be hard on the issue and soft on the people is an important people management skill.

The world health organization states that a toxic work environment where there is a lot of fear and criticism may lead to physical and mental health issues, harmful use of substance, absenteeism, and lack of productivity. On the other hand, a connection in the business environment greatly impacts productivity, quality, loyalty and it also fosters employee engagements. It is the key determinant of job satisfaction.

The intention of the person who is offering criticism may be to motivate the individual, but what happens is just the opposite. They get into the vicious cycle of blame.

Psychologist, Skinner, proved through his experiment that animals rewarded for good behavior would learn much more rapidly than if they are punished for bad behavior. This same principle is applicable to human beings.

When people are emotional, advice will not enter their mind. Actually, the mind is shut to the advice during those circumstances of tension and pressure. As Fredrich Nietzsche quotes, "We often refuse to accept the idea merely because the tone of voice in which it has been expressed is unsympathetic to us."

Feedback sessions are not only a challenge to the employee but also to the authority figure. It takes plenty of physical and mental energy, and a feeling of exhaustion sets in.

The first mission for the boss, Jacob is to establish a CONNECT with the employee, Mahesh, underlining his concern for him to achieve the wavelength and resonance.

The feelings of Mahesh are real and if understood by Jacob, would give him the right ambiance and non-threatening environment. When this is worked out psychologically, Mahesh most likely will become open to inputs given by Jacob and things may work out. When you show deep empathy toward others, their defensive energy goes down, and positive energy replaces it. That's when you can get more creative in resolving the issue.

Listening to the feeling and to working on the CONNECT is crucial in binding people and establishing a diplomatic relationship for mutual benefit.

I would like to narrate the case of Srinivasan who was an employee in a production company. He was very highly committed and a top performer. There was a sudden change in his life which not only shattered his personal life but also disturbed his job performance. His wife left him, and he was going through the divorce process. His boss, Harish, could see the difference as there was a lot of absenteeism and error in his job although Srinivasan had not shared anything with him. One day, Harish walked into Srinivasan's cabin, kept his arms around his shoulder, and told him, "It looks like something is disturbing you mentally. Let me know if I can help you in any way."

According to Srinivasan, this one connecting gesture gave him a lot of emotional strength to stand strong and bring back his focus. Here, Harish has not discussed the drop in performance. He only worked on the connect, and the rest of the things fell in place by itself.

> *"You will never forget someone who was there for you at your toughest time."*
>
> *— Kahil Gibran*

Many times, individuals visit the psychotherapist's office not only for treatment but also as he or she wishes somebody would listen to them peacefully with full concentration. More than resolving their issues, these people wish somebody would understand them in and out. Many a time, just venting gives a feeling of relief and relaxation.

Listening - The Heart of A Relationship

I had an occasion when a lady of 23 years old, Jessica, came to me and sought my time for a patient listening. Jessica openly informed me at the first instance itself that, though she has come for counseling, she does not want any therapy or advice. She was very clear she craved for somebody to share her feelings and understand her with clarity. Jessica went back to her childhood age of 9. A stranger had come to her school and informed her that her mother had called her back home. Believing him, she had gone with the stranger who took her to a haunted place and abused her sexually.

She was not able to understand what that stranger was doing with her. When she returned home, Jessica cried to her mother, Stella, about what had happened to her. Stella was taken aback by the incident and pleaded to Jessica not to tell anybody about what had happened between her and the stranger.

Whenever she tried to express her fear, Jessica was frantically stopped by the mother, who told practically to abstain from the thinking. Totally puzzled and confused, Jessica was unable to express her emotions. She experienced insecurity and fear. This caused a lot of trouble in her routine. She was not able to concentrate on her studies. She was not able to score grades. Neither was she able to converse with any of her classmates freely. She was forgetting games, fun, and playing and she was practically aloof and isolated from others.

She was getting the worst flashbacks of the stranger and the dark incident which had totally spoilt her childhood. Often she dreamt of somebody chasing her, and she was desperately trying hard to escape from the chaser. No morning was pleasant to her as she had practically lost sound sleep due to the disturbed brain. She felt absolute discomfort and never slept peacefully.

Years passed by, and though Jessica was not willing to get married, her mother compelled her to get married to Christopher. Right from the first night, whenever Christopher came near her, she was transported back to that 'haunting day in her life. She was never able to relate with him, and it created incompatibility in her married life.

When Jessica was narrating, she practically cried and wept, unable to control her emotions. She desperately hunted for ventilation to forget the worst incident that occupied her chest for a decade or more. She said it was the first time she spoke about the chaos in her life, and she felt the big burden she was carrying in her heart for years was removed, and she was feeling light.

In this case study, we observe clearly that the reason for the debacle can be attributed directly to the mother, Stella. Though the stranger has caused havoc in the life of Jessica, the main culprit is Stella, who stopped Jessica from venting out, causing trouble in her chest and brain.

Clearly speaking, if the mother Stella had given her comfort, space, a safe ambiance, and environment to listen to the feelings of Jessica, that quality time of listening would have done great things for Jessica. That would have given a soothing and healing feeling to Jessica to recovering from the incident. The quality listening time would have made a world of difference to Jessica's life, and quite obviously, she would have felt people are around her to take care and help Jessica to forget the incident and the shock and live her life peacefully.

For no fault of hers, she was punished by the stranger first and then her mother. We have all experienced situations when we wished to get a person to listen to us totally, allowing us to speak from the heart and confess about incidents which we can't reveal to anybody else.

We all crave for a person who could help us unload our feelings by providing a safe ambiance.

"One of the sincere forms of respect is listening to what another has to say."
— Bryant McGill

Our mind searches for consolidated clarity by coming out of such emotional logs, which obstruct our lives to a considerable extent. When we are heard deeply with care and acceptance, we could obviously go back to the zone of comfort to lead a normal life. The listening process with complete non-judgmental acceptance would obviously redesign our individuality for us to be confident in life.

The obstacles in our mind would be removed, and we can remove our troubling masks, whatsoever it may be and move naturally in the life. The listeners are shock absorbers which serve a therapeutic purpose.

Carl Rogers narrates, "When you listen with complete positive acceptance, it is of high therapeutic value and bestows a lot of healing for the person. This is the best way to convey acceptance, trust, and respect. When we say acceptance, it is the acceptance of the person per say. Listening is a way of conveying, I don't blame you for your feelings."

The working 'X' factor in such cases is not only listening to the facts but also giving importance to emotions and feelings. It indirectly conveys a feeling of complete acceptance which leads to self-acceptance.

Listening not only to what is said but also listening to silence with the whole body involved in the activity, adding to the effect of absolute concentration on the situation and scenario.

Meena was molested by her tuition teacher. This was affecting her psychologically and let to her overall behavior like shrinking from physical contact, not interacting with anyone, and unexplained silence. Although she was initially reluctant to open up to her mother, she could no longer take it and told the mother whatever was happening. Although her mother, Shanti's initial reaction was that of shock, she listened to Meena with absolute care and empathy. She reflected on her feelings, and she made her feel very comfortable and assured Meena of her safety and reassured her that it was not at all her fault. Once this was done, Meena felt more confident and her guilt regarding the episode vanished. She conveyed to Meena that she will make sure that her sharing with the mother will not cause any trouble to Meena.

Our spouses, children, colleagues, subordinates, friends, and family are constantly watching us, persistently observing, and studying us and judge us to find out how much we can be open and be transparent to them. They are closely analyzing us to determine how much we can accept them.

Many times, parents feel that their children are not sharing any of these feelings with them in a transparent manner. If you analyze the past, there would have been instances when the kid has come to narrate what happened to them on a particular day, be it a quarrel with a classmate or why they got low marks in the examination. The parents' reaction would not have given a positive impression to them, and they would have gone without telling what they intended to.

If parents understand children and give them time to listen to them on a day to day basis, the children won't hide important happenings in their life like having a crush on a classmate, developing a dislike towards the master, or incidents like sex abuse or any other vital happenings in their life. Fearing that the parents will judge, many children forget the transparency in their personality. Invariably, children are pushed to a remote corner to get the impression that the father or mother won't understand them and there is no point in discussing anything with them.

A boy, Suresh, hires a cycle at Rs.10/- per hour. He parks the cycle somewhere in the road, and the cycle is stolen. Suresh, fearing that his mother, Veni, would punish him, decides not to go back home. He leaves the town by bus and goes to a nearby town. There, he finds a companion, Solomon, who begs or steals food from roadside shops. Suresh learns that from Solomon and becomes a shoplifter as the months pass by. The police nab him and bring him back to his mother, Veni's place and put him in juvenile prison.

Here, instead of feeling fear of disclosing losing the cycle to the mother, had he trusted that his mother would understand and support him, this amount of damage would not have happened.

There was another similar case of a boy, Navin. He lost his parents when he was in his preschool. He was brought up by his maternal uncle. One day, when he got into some mischief at school, his teacher said that he was going to complain to his uncle. The boy, fearing punishment, avoided going home. There was a well on the way home. He just jumped into the well. A few boys saw this, and he was rescued. When asked why he did this, he looked at his uncle with fear. The uncle sobbed and hugged Navin.

A similar case of a girl, Nita, can be illustrated here. Nita was sexually troubled by her uncle. And that led her to absolute insecurity and loneliness. She was not able to be comfortable and confident around her mother, Ashwini, and communicate that to her as Nita had the perception that Ashwini may not solve the issue but aggravate it more. She also feared that she would only curse her to add to the dismay. When feelings and emotions are not properly addressed, the worst aftermaths are sure to follow. Improper handling of emotions would cause a lot of critical complications.

Unexpressed feelings and mental toxicity

> *"Unexpressed emotions will never die. They are buried alive and will come forth later in uglier ways."*
>
> *— Sigmund Freud*

Unshared feelings affect the biochemistry of individuals. Researches have revealed when we use bottling up as a strategy to cope with our own emotions or emotions of others, it expresses itself either in psychological or psychosomatic concerns. Already existing health concerns are also aggravated by the suppression of feelings.

Vidya has been married for ten years. Her relationship with her husband is highly incompatible to the extent that they very rarely talk to each other. They don't eat together or have any good times together. Although the emotional connection is very lean, he often approaches her for sex. She is very reluctant of his mechanical approach and tries to avoid it. When it is time for bed, she started developing palpitation and anxiety, which increased day by day. Over a period of time, it started showing on her skin in the form of strong infections accompanied by wounds and bleeding.

Her stress led to these symptoms, and this, in turn, caused her more stress. Close interaction with her revealed that although it was stressful, this condition was also benefitting her in the form of sex avoidance, so it became very complex to treat her, both for a dermatologist and a psychotherapist.

Children are not very articulate at venting their feelings and show them in behaviors like a drop in academics, stammering, bedwetting, and nightmares.

I observed this when Lekha brought her child with the concern that she pulls her eyebrows repeatedly. In spite of Lekha's constant efforts, she was not able to help her daughter, Shobana, stop.

Shobana is an eight-year-old kid. Her eyebrows are very scanty. Close discussion with her and also her family showed that there is a lot of parental incompatibility. There are frequent episodes of violence between her parents. Initially, whenever there were such episodes, pulling her eyebrows gave her comfort and got rid of the discomfort of the situation. Over a period of time, it became a habit. Shobana's version is that whenever the parents fought, she told herself,

"Please stop it," and pulled her eyebrows. This gave her some assurance that she was doing something about the situation which was completely out of her control. Here the anxiety of the child is shown in psychological behavior.

Non-sharing of feelings lead to perpetual sickness

So merely expressing emotions, on the whole, has a healing value. People who do not share their feelings or emotions or people who do not have anybody to listen to them are highly prone to fall into perpetual sickness, develop extraordinary stress every time, and constantly possess fear and panic in their mind. They develop a habit of anxiety causing a distressed life. There can be blasts of these feelings in other ways like anger outbursts, violent behavior, and suicidal thoughts.

Thirty-five-year-old Smitha married Subodh fifteen years back, and she has been suffering from absolute incompatibility with him. Despite her sincere and honest efforts, Smitha was not able to strike a resonance with Subodh, which led to an unhealthy relationship, crossing tolerance levels. Smitha practically reached the level of distress, disappointment, and helplessness as all her efforts were in vain. She decided to commit suicide, but when she was trying to tighten the knot while committing suicide, the bell rang. She got down from the small table on which she was standing and opened the door. Her friend, Sindhu, was standing there. She had come to give an invitation to her daughter's marriage. She sat for some time, and after she left, when she returned to the room, her mind was changed. She removed the sari she had tied to the fan, and the intense idea of suicide was dropped just by venting.

Following this, she sought psychotherapeutic help to equip herself with a better way of coping whenever there was stress and pressure A small positive outlet has changed the mindset of Smitha, and it has started working wonders in her life. There was an insight in her that an outlet of emotions helped her to perceive things from a proper perspective. Her suicidal thought had been submerged as she clearly understood that there are people who seek her company and her presence in their life. The total pressure was diffused by Sindhu coming over. Now Smitha started using healthy outlets to come out of the mounting pressures.

It is same as a chamber which has been closed for years and starts accumulating dust and germs. Similarly, when the mind is closed, and feelings are shut, it accumulates stress and disease. Feelings search for a release. Sigmund Freud calls it *catharsis*, meaning inner cleaning is nothing but the ventilation of feelings in a safe and secure environment. Many times, we do not share our deepest feelings with our loved ones fearing it may cause them stress. On the contrary, we are depriving ourselves of the warm bonding which comes with this sharing.

I would like to narrate a case of an employee who was under high stress due to a workplace conflict and work pressure. He narrated that he used to cry when alone due to misbehavior of one of his seniors. When asked if he shared this with his family, he responded that he didn't want to bother them with his stress. On the other side, his wife's version of the story was that he was detaching himself from family and refrained from being involved as he used to be earlier. He had no interest in intimacy, romance, and humor. She feels, that of late, he seems to have completely lost interest in her.

Although he is trying to protect his family from feeling stressed, the family is even more stressed due to the excessive mind reading and assumptions.

If he had shared his heart, he would have received the emotional support from the family, and they would have understood the entire scenario from a better perspective. This would have helped them to provide better support rather than blame him for being moody and cold.

Unresolved and unexpressed feelings show themselves through psychological and psychosomatic disorders. Suppression is the model of dealing with emotions in many cultures. It is a maladaptive emotion regulation strategy which leads to a cluster of psychological and psychosomatic concerns.

Many times, we observe that when people face losses like the death of loved of once, failure in relationships, or any other major loss, when they express it vigorously, the post-stress chaos is lesser. In my experience of working with villagers, when there is a death of a loved one, people beat their chest and cry profusely. They generously pour out their emotions without any inhibition. It is observed that these people recover from the loss much easier.

This was apparent during the tsunami. The community as a whole was affected, and there was nobody to give emotional support as everybody else was going through the same trauma. Many people affected by such a trauma experienced post-traumatic stress disorders like anxiety, fear, depression, insomnia, and substance abuse.

Many mental health organizations came forward to simply allow families to cry out their feelings in the presence of an empathetic listener. No therapy or consoling was required here to help people, it was just being there emotionally besides them to help them talk and grieve.

Preferring an empathetic friend to a solution suggesting friend

Imagine a situation in your life when you were going through a tough phase. Will you choose to visit a friend who could empathize with you or you will you visit a person who could give you a logical solution? You will definitely visit the friend who could give you a shoulder and provide emotional support. Our feelings need a desperate outlet. When that is done, people will look for solutions. People who are more empathetic are perceived as warm and accepting. Self-disclosure of one's real self happens, and the individual feels comfortable to remove layers of the mask he was wearing. This is the reason adolescents are more comfortable with their peers as the perception is that they can discuss anything which disturbs them, which they have not discussed with anybody else.

As a therapist, I have observed in conversations between two people, each trying to talk more than the other to express themselves. They try to outclass each other by raising their voices. Or there are situations when one person talks, the second person thinks about what he is going to say in his defense and in the process fails to listen. The second person really wants to establish, that he is more powerful in thinking and much shrewder to take decisions. In such situations, when each is trying to outsmart the other, the communication becomes a boomerang without any results. If one person takes the initiative to listen to the other person, who is the speaker and understands him, there is a high possibility that on his turn, he would have properly listened and understood. Anger, sorrow, fear, and frustrations are all emotions, and they are like champagne and settle down when expressed in a safe and healthy environment. Being empathetic is one of the great virtues of a healthy relationship.

The ability to be empathically connected, especially in challenging moments, is the finest attribute for a wonderful relationship. In contrast, the absence of this connection underlines arguments and a distressed relationship. People are prone to defensive reactions when this type of connection is absent. To make one step into the other's mind creates a healthy environment.

This ability to 'feel with' another person is to identify with them and sense what they're experiencing. It's sometimes seen as the ability to 'read' other people's emotions, or the ability to imagine what they're feeling, it's the ability to make a psychic and emotional connection with another person, and to actually enter into their mind-space. Alfred Idler's beautiful definition of empathy is, *"Empathy is seeing with the eyes of another, listening with the ears of another, and feeling with the heart of another."*

When we experience real empathy or compassion, our identity actually merges with another person's. The separateness between you and the other person fades away for that moment.

If you experience this state of connection with another person, then it's impossible to judge them or criticize them. You recoil from their experiences of suffering in the same way that you recoil from your own suffering. In fact, you feel a strong desire to relieve their suffering and aid their development.

Empathy has powerful psychological benefits too. Research shows that people who are more empathic feel more satisfied with their lives, and have better relationships. Doctors and mental health professionals whose sense of empathy is high are less likely to develop burnouts.

Just as the lack of empathy makes cruelty and oppression possible, the presence of empathy heals conflict. Use your imagination to picture how the situation looks through other people's eyes. Think about how other people's predicaments make them feel, and how their experiences mold their perceptions.

When you empathize with a person, you give them your full attention, and your frame of reference doesn't come in to picture. Giving people your full attention establishes a strong connection, which enables empathy to flow between you.

Before you condemn another person for a particular behavior, you believe there is a reason for that behavior. You strongly believe that their feelings are real and they seek to be understood.

Revathi is a factory employee married for five years and has one son. Her husband works outside and visits her only once a week. Revathy stays with her mother-in-law. Her mother-in-law takes care of her son in her absence when she goes for work. Her present concern is, although she finishes all the household work and also goes for a job, her efforts were not acknowledged by the mother-in-law. As a result, whenever her mother-in-law finds fault, she gets more and more annoyed. The present scenario is such that she doesn't talk to the mother-in-law.

I asked Revathi to put herself in the mother-in-law's place and go into the details of her life. Being there in her place, she had to try to understand what was going in her mind, how her life looks like, what is her disappointment in the relationship with you, and what is her expectation from this relationship.

Revathi took a pause and said, "I think she is looking for some kind of connect and warmth from me, which I have never been showing in this relationship."

In the above case, although the situation may remain the same, the very fact that Revathi is able to put herself into her mother-in-law's shoes helped her to understand her better. She could understand that maybe even her mother-in-law is looking for acknowledgment as she is taking up the responsibility of the home and her son in Revathi's absence.

Now she is able to have a panoramic view of the situation and may have a better perspective of the entire scenario. Putting herself into her mother-in-law's position may help her to deal with the situation in a better way. She may work on her connection with her mother-in-law instead of becoming defensive. This ability to empathize serves as a communication lubricant in the relationship, thereby encouraging collaboration rather than friction.

There was a study done to see the effect of empathy among doctors. It revealed very interesting findings. In this study, the first group of doctors were asked to have comfortable eye contact with the patients, and they were asked to cautiously paraphrase what the patients said. The second group of doctors had lesser eye contact, and no paraphrasing was done.

Results showed that the patients felt that the first group is much more competent as they trusted the first group of doctors listened to them patiently and understood their problems completely and they were much more capable of solving their problems than the second group. The prognosis was also better in the first group of patients which revealed an important fact that the approach of medical professionals towards their patients have plenty of healing values.

Sometimes, although we listen, we don't leave an impression on the talker that we were concentrating and empathizing with. That makes the talker feel confused about whether he is properly understood.

Similar to the study of medical professionals was a study on the manager, to measure the impact of their approach on employees. Here, two groups of employees were measured for job satisfaction. This was correlated with the approach of managers. The study showed that employee satisfaction was directly correlated with the approach adopted by managers. The group of employees whose managers were open, understanding, and expressed interest in the employee as a person, were more satisfied than the other group who were objective and uninvolved with employees.

Here, the differences between the employers and employees was due to non-open communication between these two groups. If open communication happens periodically between management and the employees, the morale of the workplace will be high.

This is precisely the reason that in present management policies, sufficient space is given to interactive function, celebrations, and appreciation nights.

Listening to people and understanding their feelings, makes a world of difference in the relationship.

Soma's husband, Sagar, is an eminent professor at one of the highly reputed IIT. They have not had a great bond in their relationship according to Soma, "His communication is highly robotic. He talks with one word, and the compartment which contains feeling in an individual is completely lacking in him. She said, in the initial days of their marriage when she dressed up well, she expected him to look at her and admire her. She took an effort to cook good food she looked at him keenly to read appreciation in his eyes, but he was very inexpressive.

When I see clients like Soma, there is a craving to be understood by their life partner and to mutually express feelings and exchange tender gestures with each other. Here, Sagar said that when he was a child, the only aim of his mother was to make him successful and do well in life. He was motivated for success in academics. He never thought expression and appreciation were so important in relationships. To him, everything was in place, and still, his wife was not satisfied. His version is that he provides everything essential for a luxury life and still she is not happy. He said that he is not an alcoholic or he does not abuse her or restrict her.

> *"When dealing with people, remember you ate not dealing with creatures of logic but creatures of emotions."*
>
> *— Dale Carnegie*

The ability to connect to people's feelings develop from early childhood. The observations of the child with regard to their parents and other people around make them mold the ability to connect to other person's feelings.

John Bowlby, an eminent psychologist, conducted a study on children. John Bowlby rightly asserts that intimacy and empathy are vital ingredients, giving a hypothetical net to us, which holds us strongly and prevent us from failing miserably. Not only children, even an adult need perfect bonding to feel good about himself and the world around him.

The trust in any individual makes him stronger and stronger to yield highly favorable results. This is much more essential in the formative years. If the child is not shown proper care and concern, it is a blatant fact that he would grow powerless and purposeless. If he is not listened to, not empathized with or not understood, this may have an impact on his later life.

This was very well proved in the case of Vasu given below. Vasu was brought for consultancy by his mother, Shyamala. But his father, Venkatraman, was not willing to be a part of psychotherapy. Vasu is just an average student, and he was not able to be successful in academics. Due to this, it became a common scene in their family of Vasu getting bad marks, month after month and Venkatraman beating him black and blue every time. Shyamala would try to intervene between them and also getting hit in the process by Venkatraman.

Hit marks, bruises, and scars could be seen all over face and the body of Vasu. His friends and classmates used to criticize him after each monthly test. The test, marks, punishments, and criticisms all made him dejected and disappointed. He also developed a hatred towards his father, who is the reason for this debacle of him being averse to education.

When Vasu was out to celebrate his birthday once, it was his bad luck that it coincided with his exam results and that turned out to be a painful day as he was beaten by Venkatraman with a coat hanger. It caused him a lot of bruises and scars on his head and face.

After the incident, Vasu was sent to the neighboring town to his uncle's place for studying further. His uncle, Ramchandra took the law into his own hands and was beating and punishing Vasu on a day to day basis, offering much worse of a treatment to Vasu than his father. Vasu had no other go but to stay with his uncle for almost a decade. And now Vasu is a grown up and has practically become an adult, growing taller than his father. The worst thing is even his hatred about father and uncle grew with him, and now he has become volatile, effervescent, erratic, and outrageous, unable to be controlled by anybody.

If somebody is trying to find fault or mistakes in his work, he would use arrogant words towards them and attack them if required. In a perfect sense, now it has become Vasu's goal to take revenge on his father and uncle.

When he came home to join his parents, due to his father raising the hand to hit him, Vasu found the coat hanger which his father has beaten him with a decade back and started smashing him with that. And the coincidence now is Vasu was attacking father exactly when the father was celebrating his birthday. Vasu was never bothered about the aftermath.

In the process of attacking the father, he also smashed his mother, Shyamala, who had to protect the husband from the son. In the process, her elbow was fractured, and she had to get her hand bandaged.

During therapy, Vasu said that he wanted to kill his father and his uncle. Vasu often spoke of going to prison as a punishment for attacking and killing these people in his life.

Vasu's brutal attack in a violent manner caused bruises and scars on the face of his father, and Vasu kicked, blasted, and chased him to go to the office with scars, bruises, and marks. His intention was to make his father ashamed, similar to what happen to him. He wished to see father's colleagues making fun of Venkatraman about his bruises and scars. Such was the vengeance that Vasu developed from Venkatraman.

This study of Vasu's case would have revealed how normal children became outrageous due to their childhood experiences. Instead of punishing Vasu, if Venkatraman had connected with Vasu and sat for a discussion with Vasu about the issues, he is facing in studies, things would have been different. This connect would have moved their relationship in the affirmative direction.

The roots of this understanding and empathy are formed in the early years and show in all relationships. Sigmund Freud talks about the *indissoluble bond*. This bond, he says, is an invisible umbilical cord which inherits the feeling of care and nurturing.

The development of a secure base is crucial to develop the perfect connect, which is the right origin for any communication.

One mother consciously taught her child the value of understanding the other person's feelings. Whenever she noticed someone suffering from pain, food deprivation, and loss, she asked her child, "What you think he must be feeling now?" She allowed the child to feel and express.

It is easily imbibed when learned in childhood than at a later stage.

Longing for acknowledgment

My clients, Sneha and Deepak, who learned the significance of putting oneself into the other person's shoe in a hard way. Sneha is a homemaker. She takes care of the household and the children all by herself. Deepak has long working hours and barely gets the time. Most of the time, the indirect message conveyed by Deepak is that his contribution to the family is more valuable than hers.

As time went by, Sneha started more and more complaining of her routine and pressure of multiple responsibilities. Whenever she did that, he responded with much more vigor, pointing out his work pressure and her flaws. Such conversations used to be mentally tiring and ruin the entire day. Here, Deepak is perceiving Sneha's complains as a personal attack and starts attacking her to defend himself. All he wanted was to fix things. In this case, Sneha is longing to be acknowledged and appreciated. When it is not done by Deepak, she reacts even more furiously.

As Deepak is adopting defense as a technique to combat this argument, it was not working out. In fact, it was leading to more and more problems. Once, Deepak held her hand and told her, "I am wondering how you are able to manage so many responsibilities." He observed, to his astonishment, that she immediately mellowed down. This led to a paradigm shift, and Deepak understood that it an unmet need of Sneha to feel understood and significance which has been triggering her.

This led Deepak to acknowledge, attend, and appreciate her efforts. When Deepak was doing this, Sneha also was conveying similar messages to him. Earlier, they were both pointing out their contributions and efforts for the family, but now it is the other way. This led to a lot of nourishing in the relationship.

Here And Now

During heated conversations, or to be precise, during arguments, we observe volatile outbursts from both the parties due to issues that have passed by. Both parties rake up issues of the past, and due to that, the very conversation becomes a blame cycle. Such blame cycles are endless. In those circumstances, the current issue, for which a solution has to be found would suffer because the past-blame cycle becomes very vicious and hard to handle. It becomes self-perpetuating, and the other person is also pulled into the cycle. Instead of such arguments, trekking back to the past, if both parties decide and discuss only the current issue, a worthy solution can be procured.

On the contrary, if even one of the two talks about the past, bigger controversies would occur between both and the very purpose of dialogue, to solve the current issue, would be defeated. Mutually blaming one and other about the past leads to character criticism from both the parties. And we tend to generalize and end up making judgments about the person.

Out mind is trained to think and communicate in terms of what is right and what is wrong with people. When we do this, we end up becoming judgmental and evaluative. This reaction is habitual.

Our initial response to a conflicting situation is more primitive and emotional. That is, we either attack in the form of judgment or we try to sulk. Many times, this habitual and automatic response causes a lot of guilt later. Here, to be conscious about our reactions and wait until we are able to operate with a rational response is very crucial. When we are emotional, our mind is readily able to locate critical and blaming scenarios from the past. Here, we tend to choose words which are more evaluative than factual. In this state of mind, a person generally complains rather than ask for what he needs.

HERE AND NOW communication is a healthy approach to a relationship. It assures greater authenticity, increased understanding, deep connection, and better conflict resolution. It emphasizes, consciously staying in the present and being focused on the issues. This approach shares power with others rather than use it to suppress someone. Here, the communication is clear, empathetic, and in the present.

Here, the needs are clearly specified without being demanding, critical, or judgmental. The emphasis is on consciously staying in the present. It focuses on observations which are specific to time, place, and context. The needs are clearly specified. For example, *you never spend time with me.* Now, this statement has an element of generalization and is more likely to evoke a defensive reaction. In this statement, the need is not specified clearly. The alternative will be *I want you to spend time with me more often.* Here, the need is clear, and the context is in the present.

A mother is telling the kid that he is wasting a lot of time watching TV If she opts to quote the immediate facts, hinting to the kid, that he or she has been viewing TV from 11.00 a.m. to 3.00 p.m. the event day, it works out being a better mode for addressing the issue.

Although it is right, either of these methods may not guarantee the desired results. Definitely, the second method on the HERE AND NOW model, would obviously yield much better result as it won't offend the kid.

The HERE AND NOW model is more specific. Instead of generalizing, for example, "You are always very late." If we say we were supposed to meet by 11 am today, and it is 12.30 p.m. the concerned person would immediately accept the point you are trying to make. In this example, the facts are observable, clear, and in the present.

When you take up the issue by generalizing a person is a latecomer, the issue may take different unwanted directions and proportions, leading to hatred and complications in the relationship.

Let us analyze a situation hypothetically when a conversation is happening. When a person is talking and the second person is not seeing him directly and looking here and there without looking at the speaker, obviously it leads to confusion in the speaker.

Usually, the first person would tell the second person, "You never show interest in whatever I say." But in the HERE AND NOW model, it is the action which has just happened. "I see that you are looking here and there when I am talking to you."

Here, the listener cannot object spontaneously as you are quoting a fact on recent observation and not on a foregone conclusion, which relates to the judging of the personal character of the listener. This way of the refined HERE AND NOW approach may not offend the person as he can't deny what you have said. Similarly, instead of telling a person by questioning him "Why are you shouting?" if you tell him, "You are raising your voice," this is a fact and not your evaluation.

In a hypothetical scenario, a husband is late, and the wife is worried. She tries calling him, and there is no response from him. She gets very restless worrying about him. Just then he comes home, she starts getting furious, and he responds with intense anger. Here, the core feeling of the wife was that of 'concern for him' but it was expressed as anger. She could have mentioned her true feelings for e.g, "I was worried about you when you did not answer the call." Here the feeling is genuinely conveyed. She further continues, "You inform me hereafter if you are going to be delayed." Here, the need is very clear.

Researches show that the HERE AND NOW approach to giving feedback is much effective, pleasing, and productive as the purpose of the feedback is to strengthen the relationship.

In work situations, we come across situations, where we observe the consequences of employer-employee feedback sessions. Sometimes, the relationships go haywire after such sessions, and they develop anger and hatred towards the employer.

If FEEDBACKS are not conducted effectively, they miss the vital points of such sessions, defeating the very objective of the feedback sessions. Instead of striving for growth, these kind of meetings reduce the morale of the employees. This is similar to a teacher who highlights a mistake with red ink and overlooking achievements.

It is very important to talk about measurable information in your description of behavior. It should lead to clarity of behavior, which leads to growth. What is crucial here is working on observable facts than past assumptions.

For executing this, what is really needed is a clear and transparent mental makeup. It is required that you observe and watch what is currently happening and record the observations on what you see, what you hear, and what actually happens physically.

If we hold back our past analysis, judgment, evaluation, and diagnosis and work more with the

HERE AND NOW, it may yield finer results. In case the manager has to give feedback on the PUNCTUALITY of all his team members, instead of saying, "You are always later to the office," if he practically observes this behavior, he can authentically quote ascertained facts with feedbacks quoting as follows. "For the past three days, I see that you are coming, by 10 a.m instead of 9 a.m." The manager can go further by also being specific in feedback, and on what he expects from his team members like- "In case you are going to be delayed, please call up and inform."

With this approach, we get space for negotiation and open the door for communication with clarity to achieve the desired results.

The Impact of Communication on Chemical Changes

When a group of managers underwent research, the impact of conversation on chemical changes was revealed. While two groups of the managers were selected to impart feedback to the employees. Both the groups of managers adopted a different approach to giving feedback. One group was more accepting and empathetic, while the other group was critical. Post feedback, the first group of participants were in a positive frame of mind and were better motivated whereas the second group of participants were not.

Here, in the feedback session, people got disgusted not only by mere criticism but also the method of attack.

Chemistry plays a vital role when we are criticized, and on rejection, our bodies produce a higher level of cortisol, a hormone that impacts the thinking center of the brain. Appreciation, acceptance, and solution focused words and phrases produce oxytocin and feel good hormones. Communication experts, Dr. Andrew Newberg and Mark Roberts, suggest that when positive words are utilized, the motivational center of the brain gets activated. On the other hand, when negative words are used, we are preventing certain positive chemicals from being produced.

This contributes to stress management. A single negative word can release stress chemicals both to the speaker and to the listener. Negative words are more powerful, and they have a very high impact. For every negative word, a number of positive words are required to combat the effect. If anger and displeasure are expressed in solution-focused positive words, it is much more effective. Merely seeing positive words like love, peace, and harmony can have the impact of relaxing. We commonly observe that people who use positive words in their vocabulary have greater emotional regulations.

Studies reveal that when people spoke about the POSITIVE aspect of a situation or a person, they were more relaxed than when they spoke often about negative aspect. We observe that in our life when we constantly focus and talk about the negatives of people, event and situation, it causes the feeling of being drained away mentally.

Brain scan research shows that by visualizing or meditating on positive words, thoughts, and feelings, the outcome can be more powerful. The constant use of hostile words has a very damaging impact on our brain.

In one of the major studies, groups of adults were asked to write three things which went well throughout the day. This was done for three months, and results showed that their level of happiness improved and it continued even when people stopped writing. This can be a guideline for parents, managers, and teachers.

Awareness of One's Own Communication – Crucial in Conversation

A very crucial aspect of communication is our awareness of our own communication. Many a time when we talk, listeners understand more than what we talk. We are only aware of the words that we are conveying, but the other person is able to read the communication in total. Words can be altered, tilted, and manipulated. But the body and language convey a lot more. Your intonations, gestures, postures, eye conveyance, add much more than what you say and people obviously believe more than what you really say.

When the body language differs from what is said, people believe the body language, and the words tend to lose their meaning.

Hence, it is really important to be aware of one's body language.

Parents invariably say and affirm to children that they trust them when they actually have fears about their social life. This fear is somehow sensed by the child.

By observing people who come for therapy, a lot is communicated through body language. People who come for consultations, on their first visit, would practically sit on the edge of the chair with their arms and body closed. This shows their discomfort in opening up and initiating conversation. This is the clue that the comfort level needs to be developed.

Here, the initial objective of any therapist is to make the person more comfortable and relaxed. Once the client understands that the therapist is open, transparent, and accepting, they obviously relax in the chair, showing comfort, and there are a lot of gestures showing openness.

I have come across a senior person, Mr. Ranganath, who proclaims, he is really open to take others' view. But in reality, when the other persons start expressing their view, he would gesture with his palms to stop their talking, Though he says he is open to other peoples' ideas, His gesture conveys just the opposite.

People are really offended by such double standards of people Mr. Ranganath. And he is often wondering what aspect of him makes the other person be away from him.

Reciprocity – Law of Social Psychology

The law of reciprocal relationship is a law of social psychology, It basically says, "If someone does some good thing to us, we would have a deep rooted urge to reciprocate in some form or other. If somebody does nice things to us, we get an automatic urge to do something nice to them in return. Negative reciprocity is the action that has a negative effect that is returned with another negative effect. If one person is violent, the other will return with similar violence.

A couple who came for therapy consultation spoke to me in turns. First, the husband, Jacob, submitted his version, hinting that there is no great significance in their relationship as she follows the guidance of her sister for anything and everything. His complaint was that she does not even consider to take his consent to do anything as all her decisions are influenced by her sister's opinion.

On her turn, the wife, Philomena, complained that the husband was not at all bothering to spend time with her. She also added as her sister, Catherine, was able to absorb her feelings and spend considerable time for her, she is lined up with her totally.

Both the husband and wife, Jacob and Philomena, took their time to bring up all the allegations about each other, expressing their disappointments after their marriage, quoting many instances one after the other

When they were asked to narrate any good happenings in their life, Jacob thought for a while and began eulogizing Philomena for being affectionate and welcoming of his family. Philomena, on her narration of the positives of Jacob, was in all praise for his great concern for her parents and the amount of respect he gave to them.

She even quoted an incident when her father was practically struggling with a huge financial burden. During that time, it was Jacob who came to rescue of his father in law and saved him from all his financial travails. When Jacob expressed openness in working out certain things from his side, Philomena also expressed the openness to change.

Philomena rounded off her submission saying that Jacob is basically very nice, except for the few characteristics which are really glaring.

She finally concluded that they will have a heart to heart discussion and sort out their differences and issues amicably. When Philomena took the responsibility of working out differences, Jacob too took the responsibility.

What is prominent in this case study is visibility and the law of RECIPROCITY. When one person started with complaints, the other also continued in the same line, and when one started with a compliment, the other did the same. They were reciprocating both positives and negatives.

In any relationship, when one person is involved in fault finding, the other develops a natural tendency to do the same. This is an unconscious process and has a vast impact on the relationship.

This is what happens in real life. In a social gathering, when we give a compliment to somebody, a similar compliment boomerangs.

Similarly, when you put the blame on somebody, he will return the blame to you. Most of us do not consciously think about reciprocity in our intimate relationships.

Many times a perceived rivalry, although it may not be a real rivalry, boomerangs a real rivalry. When one person in the family perceives being rejected, they tend to respond with alienation and rejection.

Many a time, people say that they fear their own anger. Here, what they actually fear is the anger of the other person which is going to come as a response to this person's anger. Deep down in our subconscious, we know what we give in an interpersonal relationship will come back with the same force.

Small Things Matters in Relationship

Great relationships evolve out of a series of small things

A minister's wife had a huge house, many servants, n-number of cars, and all the worldly amenities to celebrate life. But despite all this, she was craving for something. Every evening she takes the car and goes to small hutment areas nearby where people with daily wages dwell.

She used to park the car at a distance and observe how they spend their evenings. Men come back tired after their hard work. Wives and husbands discussed what has happened on the day and children await the arrival of the father for chatting, playing, and eating together.

The minister's wife keenly used to observe all the evening happenings, how the family was taking up the perennial issue of the day, and how they arrive at a solution for the same.

There also used to be scenes of fighting and quarreling between the husband and wife when they discuss some issues. However, she used to observe how soon they resolved them and came to normalcy. She admired the way they took care of any house repair work on their own, how they counted their daily earnings and allocated money for the next day's expenses.

The minister's wife used to utter, "I always place myself in their place and enjoy the happenings." She imagined entering into their shoes and living their lives. She always feels that although they are in poverty, she too is in poverty of those small things which added flavor to life.

When we think about our past, we tend to reminisce about small happenings with others.

A child, Abdul, was not so great when it was academics. He was a child with very low self-esteem. One day he was made to perform on the stage for an event. Just when he came down from the stage, his class teacher smiled and put her affectionate hands around his shoulder. This one thing meant tons of appreciation for him, and he said that this was a turning point in his life. This one small gesture motivated him, and he became more and more focused and committed.

It may have happened in our own lives. Remember a winter day when you are totally chilled out and practically shivering in the cold and in a deep sleep, someone comes with a woolen blanket and wraps your body. Nobody can rule out the feelings which come with such gesture. This cannot be replaced by anything.

While in a marriage, we are engrossed in doing many major things like building a house, accumulating money for the future, the safety of the family, the education of the children, but when analyzed, incompatibility most of the time is due to the ignorance of small, tiny, and tender gestures which may serve as lubricant.

When tiny warm gestures are missing, they begin to cause stiffness in the relationship. Within a relationship when people convey tender feelings through small things, big jerks are survived.

A couple had approached counseling due to severe incompatibility. The lady felt completely disconnected from him. She said his conversation was only centered on materials and money saving. He never expressed gestures of romance or love. When probed further, it was found that the marriage was not consummated. When the husband was asked to reflect on this issue, he said he wanted to work on building a house and a future, the marriage could be consummated any time.

Small sharings, cute, humorous moments, chilling out on late evenings, looking keenly and listening to one another, laughing together on silly things, convey multiple messages of care. These serve as very big positive factors for binding relationships.

I have come across a husband fighting for conjugal rights. In the course of legal proceedings, he said "Yes, of course, we fought tooth and nail, no doubt. Every day practically... But I cannot forget the care and concern she has shown on me. I can't forget the days when I did not even have time for my breakfast and how she took care and walked around me for feeding me. These thoughts are hovering around me, creating a guilty feeling within me."

During my factory visits, on my rounds of employee counseling, I came across a woman laborer, Parvathi. During a counseling session, I was practically shocked to see the number of bruises, nail marks, and scars in her body. There were also a number of surgery stitches in many parts. Parvathi confessed that she had also undergone a lot of bone fractures.

All these were caused by her drunkard husband, Marudhu, who comes back home after heavy drinking of alcohol. It is an everyday scene at their home. Immediately, on arrival to the home, Marudhu would torture Parvathi and manhandle her and her two children. Understandably, all the evenings proved to be curses for her and children, and they were practically scared to be at home during the evenings.

During one on one therapy, I saw a big swelling on Parvathi's face. When asked about that, Parvathi said it was routine in her married life, and she was invariably undergoing those travails of torture every day. When questioned why she was still persisting to live the life in such abusive relationship, Parvathi categorically outlined that, she would forget the worst Marudhu had done to her when she recalled tiny, pleasant gestures Marudhu had made.

She said, "When I was sick and unwell, Marudhu cooked food for me, fed me time to time and bothered to give the right medicine at the right time without even making a small fuss. On those days of sickness, Marudhu only took care of the children. When I developed a hatred towards eating, due to bitterness in the mouth due to medicines, Maruthu only sat with me and insisted that I should certainly eat and practically fed me." More than the food, Maruthu's caring gestures always swirl around in Parvathi's mind, and that was vividly transparent during the therapy

Parvathi also expressed how she was morally down when her mother expired and how Marudhu took care of their suffering family. When she was very depressed, his caring hands were around her shoulders.

The single tiny gesture meaning, I AM WITH YOU, has a huge significance in the relationship. It survived heavy jerks within the relationship.

I have seen small misunderstandings at a tender age between siblings, and I have also seen how that small misunderstanding keep them separated throughout their lives. And the worrying factor is these small misunderstanding would have been caused because of very small things done unintentionally.

During one of the training session for police official, a deputy superintendent, Mary, narrated her own life story, which may be apt to illustrate here when we discuss small things that happened in childhood. Mary and his sister, Helen, were doing their schooling. Though Mary's performance was average, Helen was a topper in the class.

Mary could recall a time when she was asked to help her mother with household work, and Helen was asked to sit and study. Her mother's version was that Helen was sincere in studies and was aspiring to be a medical student. This caused a lot of hurt and the feeling of being discriminated. The cause of this according to Mary was Helen. This started to cause a rift between both of them which continued even after decades.

Now, Helen has become a surgeon and Mary is a police officer. But the hurt from the childhood continues.

The childhood gap created unknowingly by small things from the parents have widened so much, and it has practically created a separation between the two of them.

As a family counselor, I have observed that gestures like looking at each other, smiling, sharing, and spending time, which are lubricants in the relationship have drastically gone down as people spend more time with virtual people than with people who are present closer. It is a common scenario that in the restaurants, beaches, and other places, although families are together, everybody is engrossed in their mobiles, and there is deadly silence between people. Certain crucial aspects of relationships are jerked due to this. This as a contributing factor to the incompatibility and lack of intimacy in the relationship.

A research study conducted at Virginia Tech showed that the quality of conversation is high when mobiles are not around than with mobiles around.

It is not the use of mobile but the misuse of mobile which cause damage.

Carry Home Message From the Chapter

A connect is the beginning of any communication. Any negotiation if at all is possible, is possible with the perfect connect.

Focus on here and now and talk only about it, be specific be in the present, be non-judgmental…

Your actions and your words boomerang.

Positive words bring well-being, and negative words bring stress.

Small things are a huge deal in a relationship.

Your body speaks more than words.

PART - 3

Attention – A
Therapeutic Tool

"Attention is the rarest and purest form of
generosity."

– Simone Weil

Giving attention is the most basic form of love. Deep empathetic listening is the strongest form of attention and is a strong instrument in conveying, I value you... I love you...

Following the initial sessions in counseling, people generally feel that their confidence level has got elevated when they are given complete attention. This conveys the message that what you say is valuable, and enhances their self-esteem. Although the therapist would not have done anything technical, a complete conscious listening and by itself would have served as a therapeutic effect.

According to neuropsychology, when we practice deep listening, the amygdala of the person speaking and the hippocampus of the person listening cools down. I have observed in my decades of practice that failing to pay attention in the relationship is the topmost cause of relationship breakdown. Many times, although within the family, people are with each other, they do not pay attention to each other rather they spend more time with gadgets.

Attention is used by psychotherapists as a therapeutic tool. The principle behind this is that *when total and complete quality attention is given to some act, the chances that it will be repeated to the next level will be higher*

When the child is doing something enthusiastically, for example, speaking, working, or drawing, when it is given attention, it is increased and strengthened. This is seen in the following case study of a child.

A three-year-old child was not speaking. Both the parents were working and did not have time to be with the child. The caretaker did not talk to the child. It was alarming for the parents to know that their lack of stimulation was the key reason for the child not improving in speech and they consciously began to spend time, paying attention to the child whenever the child babbled and speech improved within few months. Healthy stimulation serves as an attention tool and is very crucial during the early stages of development. A similar case of a child who is ten years and still used baby talk. When observed keenly, it was found that the parents admired the child when he spoke and this served as a reward for the child, and the baby talk continued. This maladaptive behavior continued until the parents consciously became aware. When attention is given to this behavior, the child develops the thought that I count only when I am involved in these behaviors.

The preschool years are formative years, and teachers attention play a vital role both in psychological growth of the child and correction of behavioral problems like isolation, lethargy, aggression, and also regressive behavior like crawling. Sometimes a very small amount of positive attention is sufficient to motivate the child. As the children grow into adolescents, the main source of attention is the peers.

Unfortunately, we pay attention to negative behaviors like temper tantrums, adamant behavior, sickness, and these behaviors increase. Responses like shooting, threatening, interrogation, and lecturing are not punishments but are rewards. When children, and sometimes adults, do not get attention in a positive way, they try to get it in any way they can.

A women realized that her husband paid attention only when she communicated by shouting and, over a period of time, developed the habit of shouting and stopped communicating politely as whenever she tried to communicate politely, she was not attended to.

Data from Gallops shows that

+ if a manager criticizes his subordinates, then disengagement grows to 25% and people who work for that manager feel sick.

+ If the manager ignores them, disengagement grows by 45%.

+ If the manager notices a single strength and appreciate that strength, disengagement falls to less than 1%, and people stay healthy.

Giving unpleasant or negative attention will not eliminate the behavior; rather it strengthens it. The intensity of the reaction and the reliable immediate response are most effective in making a behavior occur again.

Give attention to behavior that you want to see again, catch people doing good things and appreciate it. Children crave for attention. If you show approval by giving focused and meaningful attention which can be verbal or a subtle nonverbal gesture to constructive behavior, they will repeat those behaviors. Most of the time, we wear magnifying glasses to search for behavior which needs to be corrected rather than search for behavior to be appreciated.

The opposite to attention is **Ignore**. If maladaptive behaviors are ignored, and without an audience, these behaviors most likely will fall down.

Ignore techniques work well when you have a healthy relationship and when you have been giving positive attention to the healthy behavior of an individual. If the quota of attention for the approved behavior is not given, ignoring as a technique may not work, and in fact, it may backfire. Russell Barkley quotes that, "Kids who need the most love will ask for it in the most unloving way."

A balance of attention and ignore techniques are used in therapy to treat behavioral problems in children and sometimes adults. Take the case of a child who falls sick very often. Parents panic whenever the child shows some symptoms. His behavior increased as the child grew and started to use his sickness as a factor to draw attention from parents. Many times, even between couples, sickness is highly reinforced. They do not give attention to the health and healthy behavior of the partner, and so sickness is unconsciously utilized to draw attention and care.

Whatever is given attention tends to become stronger. A hypothetical scenario- A child asks the mother to get the toy and throws a temper tantrum and finally starts rolling himself on the floor. The mother feels humiliated and decides to accept the demand made by the child. Here, the mother has created a learning in the child that if I roll on the floor, my mother would certainly give in to the demand. So here, rolling on the floor is reinforced by the mother and now the probability that the child does it more often has increased. On the contrary, if she had just ignored this behavior by neither giving positive attention nor giving negative attention, he would have settled after some time.

Attention to any attitude ascends in proportion

It is common to see aggression, temper outbursts, sulking, and sarcasm increase when attended to. On the contrary, if these behaviors are just ignored, and healthy behavior and healthy open communication is given attention, it obviously develops.

Attention is the strongest reward. When you give complete attention to the behavior or act of the other person, it is more likely to increase.

This was demonstrated by an experimental study by a group of school psychologists. A child by name Ann was only interacting with adults and not interacting with h peers. The study was aimed to help Ann develop more interaction with her peers.

Here, adults were given instructions to give attention to Ann in the form of looking at her, smiling at her, and patting her only when she interacted with peers. The results of the study were periodically tested to find the efficacy of this attention. It was found that her interaction with her peers increased gradually.

To test the validity of the experiment, it was reversed. Now the guideline adults were instructed to give attention to her if she interacted only with adults and this made Ann interact more with adults. Correspondingly, Ann's interaction with the peers reduced drastically.

The same principle is used in therapy for the treatment of other behavioral issues among children. The following case illustrates the common issues which we come across among children that are brought for therapy. A child was brought for therapy by his mother on the complaint of adamant behavior.

The mother told the therapist that he makes sure he gets his way. When the therapist asked the mother what happened when she was not heeding to his demands, the mother said he was banging his head on the floor, and she had to run to stop him and heed his demands. Thus the manipulative behavior of the child is paid and reinforced. Here, the mother was instructed to replace attention with the simple ignore technique, although it was going to be very difficult. Here, the child's behavior is just ignored as if it does not do anything to the mother in any way and the healthy behavior was given attention. When he stopped getting paid for the maladaptive behavior, it stopped.

Psychological therapies are based on a principle that any behavior which is appreciated, attended and rewarded will continue. And in contrast, any behavior which is not attended to and ignored will recede in the intensity and slow down or even go to the extent of nonexistence. This was clearly shown by B.F. Skinner in his experiment with the keyboard and pigeons. The pigeons pressing a particular key increased as it was rewarded with bestowing of food pallets. For human beings, a very strong appreciation and reward is attention.

This was experimentally demonstrated by a very popular study by name monster study that was conducted by Wendell Johnson at the University of Iowa. The name 'monster' is negative because of the unethical methods that were used to determine the positive and negative approaches of children.

Wendell Johnson of the University of Iowa selected twenty-two orphaned children. Some of them were stuttering, and some were okay. Both groups of children were told that they are going to be placed for speech therapy sessions to improve their fluency.

The group of children who were stuttering were placed in positive speech therapy, and they were praised for their fluency. The other group of children who were not stuttering were placed in negative speech therapy, and they were pulled down and disparaged for every grammatical mistake. Sessions were going on in this format for both the groups.

As a result of this experiment, children who received negative speech therapy suffered psychological effects and developed speech problems. They became self-conscious and were very reluctant to speak. After decades of this experiment, when these participants were located and assessed, it was found that the damage was still persisting. There was an unrepairable scar on their personality.

Wendell was highly criticized for not doing anything to reverse the condition. Although after decades, the University had to pay compensation to the group which suffered due to this experiment.

One time, I came across parents who were highly stressed as their four-year-old daughter was stammering. I observed that each time the daughter stammered, both the parents started correcting her. Here, the stammering was given attention and not fluency. As the parents were giving attention and correcting the words which the child was stammering, the child became more and more conscious, and the stammering increased. Here the parents were advised to just ignore the stammering of the daughter and pay attention to the daughter when she was talking without correcting or without prompting her with the words. The child's fluency improved gradually.

Focussing on negative aspects forces negative results

As parents, teachers, and caretakers, we do the same damage knowingly or unknowingly. Most of the time our focus is on behavior which needs to be corrected, and we do not pay attention to the majority of behavior which is already in place.

Psychological studies have been done on people with a good general well-being, and it was found that a mixture of positive and negative events takes place in an individual's life. The individual who focuses on happy events which have happened in his life, most probably remains in a positive frame of mind and, here, the chances of him coming across a positive event in his life will be higher.

An individual who gives more attention to the negative events in life is more likely to remain in a negative frame of mind, being low and gloomy. When people approach a therapist for relationship difficulty, one common factor which is observed is that they focus most of the time on the negative and non-workable aspects of each other. This leads to plenty of frustration and helplessness.

The role of the therapist is to draw their attention to factors which are already in place and the factors which are workable. When they start doing this consciously, on their own, in their day to day life, things become better. The core here is shifting the perspective to the more positive aspects of life and a relationship. This becomes a vicious cycle. Paying attention to positive aspects and ignoring the negative events is the essence of positive psychology.

Psychogenic or patients pretention

Thiry-two-year-old year Rajeswari got married seven years earlier to Ravi who is not so expressive, mainly due to professional pressures. His profession demands abundant time and adequate concentration. Rajeswari was feeling lonely as her husband was not able to spend time with her on a regular basis.

Even after he came home, he would be busy with his laptop and cell phone. Rajeswari rarely remembers a time when she spent time with Ravi in the warmth, love, and fun in their relationship. Whenever she approached Ravi, he used to say that he is slogging with work only for Raji and her children.

One day, Rajeswari suffered fits and went unconscious. Ravi desperately took her to hospitals and all the medical examinations were done to check all the health parameters and diagnose the illness. But despite the treatment, she suffered fits incessantly and perpetually. The frequency of the attacks was increasing week after week.

Ravi became much more tense because of this, and he was concerned more about Raji's health. He did all the assessments required to find out the nature of the problem. Meanwhile, he was completely concentrating on her health and well-being.

Immediately, on reaching the office also, he would think about Raji's health and enquire her about her wellness. Disturbed by her health, Ravi used to rush back home, sit with her, and take care of her.

All the medical reports were checked by specialists, and they confirmed that there was absolutely no physiological cause for these frequent fits.

The neurologist suggested that she take the psychologist's guidance and assessment to find the root cause. During the counseling session, there were discussions with Rajeswari, Ravi, and parents about Rajeswari, individually and separately, to conclude their analysis on Raji's illness.

The studies clearly landed upon the inference that Raji's case was predominantly a psychogenic case, where she feels really left alone, and there is a big void of attention in her. These void had caused a lot of anxiety for Rajeswari, and that became the root cause for her suffering through incessant fits. Her subconscious mind has catalyzed to create anxiety into physical symptoms which helped her to fill the void.

This condition is as real as neurological fits, and everything is happening on a subconscious level, and it has to be treated with the same seriousness as organic symptoms. The patient, Raji, is not aware about this phenomenon consciously, and it amounts to be a reality.

Sometimes, when we conclude that such cases are psychogenic, people tend to think that the patient is pretending. But that is not the case. The patient is unaware of what is happening to her.

Although this condition has to be handled with care, the psychologist has to put a lot of concentrated effort into it. A lot of high-quality time and attention is needed by the psychologist along with the family and Raji for a symptom-free phase.

In many such cases and cases where there is actually a real sickness, there is a secondary gain. *Secondary gain* is a psychological gain. It is the advantage that occurs secondary to the stated or real illness. Fitting into this sick role may have some incidental, secondary gain for the patient. Most of the time, after missing the love and affection, such sickness works out like magic, and it resolves the basic issue of regaining love and affection from the loved ones.

The role of the psychologist here is to keenly observe the gain which the individual is receiving and which is sustaining the sickness. A perfect blend of attention and ignoring have to be planned with the patient and also the family as a whole.

Even in a day to day life, without being consciously aware, we bring down the adaptive behavior and strengthen the maladaptive behavior. I have commonly heard women say they are interested in cooking and dressing, but over a period of time, when she feels that it is not acknowledged, she loses interest. Many times a small facial gesture serves as an attention tool.

Several times, we come across people who overemphasize the drawbacks of the person in the relationship and overlook positive aspects. The aim of therapy is to draw their attention to the positive aspects of the person and the relationship.

It is not uncommon to see that when one of the children is sickly and parents are worried about him and busy attending to him, the other child feels ignored and may get involved in behavior which will get him attention from significant others.

If you don't give attention to what you love today, don't ask where it went tomorrow.

Carry Home Message
From the Chapter

Give attention to the behavior you want to see often, positive or negative.

PART - 4

A Word on Parenting

CREATING A CORDIAL CONDUCIVE ATMOSPHERE THROUGH CLEAR COMMUNICATION

Communication between a parent and a child is the bottom line in the relationship; it decides the child's adaptation to the world outside his home. Creating the right atmosphere of love, care, and discipline for the parents themselves and for the child is a large part of parenting. Listening to the child is a crucial aspect of it. When you do this, you will start looking at the issue from the frame of reference of the child rather than becoming judgmental.

A belief that the child has the potential and capacity is very crucial. It is essential that their resources are evoked in handling life issues. For example, when the child tells you, "I do not have any good friends," our immediate tendency will be to give answers. But if you listen to the child and trigger the child to find out what the child thinks is a barrier to having good friends, he will come out with workable strategies.

If the child fails, rather than advising, evoking his creative mind to think how this failure can be worked out is very important. The role of the parent is like that of a farmer. His role is to create a healthy environment to help and support the child at every stage. We need to understand the milestones at every stage. Just like physical milestones which are clearer and obvious, there are psychological milestones.

At every stage of development, their needs and behaviors are different, which is normal for that age, but which may not be normal for other age. When the child is small, his interpretation is very concrete, and his thinking is very simple and direct. His understanding of the world around him is very literal. When told something, he cannot read between the lines.

When a three-year-old child took another child's toy, his mother got annoyed and became very worried thinking that her child has learned to steal. Actually knowledge of property rights does not develop until early childhood. It only meant that her child liked the other's kid toy and he had taken it. Parents can make the child return the toy by talking and explaining to the child that the toy with which he is playing is not his toy and it belongs to the other kid.

As the child's thinking is very concrete, he would understand the situation literally. When the mother keeps the newborn child closer to herself, the elder child's interpretation will be that the parents like his younger sibling more. With the child already having such feelings, everything the parent does will be seen in this light. Even the slight raising of voice may cause a feeling of being discriminated.

A child studying in fourth class, Anushka, is an academically high performer and also is socially popular in her class. And all of a sudden, she is reluctant to go to school and practically refuses to go to school. When she was forced by parents to go to school, she went in panic, unable to understand what was happening. The class teacher sends Anushka back home. Despite the efforts by the teacher to make her comfortable and to let her say what has troubled her and why she gets disturbed, Anushka was not able to come back to her normal self.

The teacher desperately tried to provide a friendly atmosphere, so that Anushka would become normal. It did not help her, and the teacher had no other go but to send her back home.

A detailed discussion with the parents revealed that a few months back, Anushka's father, Ashok, and her mother, Sheela, fought about some issue. During the fight, Sheela had yelled that she would commit suicide by pouring kerosene on her body and burning herself. Anushka and her brother held the feet of their mother, pleading with her not to do that. Although everything was settled, the effect of this incidence went deep in her mind.

Anushka's mind was only thinking about the incident of the fight between Ashok and Sheela and the aftermath. Her fear of losing Sheela was not allowing her to be on her own and she practically lost interest in everything. Whenever she comes out from home, she develops a panic that her mother may commit suicide. She thought that she would rescue mother if she is with her and this caused her anxiety whenever she moved away from mother, even to go to the school.

We come across refusal to go to school among children who have a recently born sibling. The child refuses to go to school due to the fear and insecurity that all the maternal love and attention will be stolen by the younger one. Hence, it is imperative and a must for parents to keep the communication channels open. Giving free space for easy interaction would only make the children comfortable to converse very freely with them. Even an iota of fear may not yield a proper result in parenting. Only if children are allowed to question every issue can the communication doors remain open between parent and child.

Many times, the typical advice of a parent given to the child may do more harm than good. The case which is narrated below is a classic example.

A lady, Josephine, lost her husband, Samuel, and they had two daughters. The elder daughter, Stella, got married to Christopher long back and the younger daughter, Isabella, was just twelve years old. All of a sudden, Josephine decided to go and stay with Stella and her husband Christopher along with Isabella.

Christopher was asking Isabella to go and buy cigarettes for him. On one such occasion, Isabella refused to go to the shop as the teenagers around the shop were making fun of her. Christopher was not able to take this refusal properly and complained to Josephine that she was not obeying her. Josephine scolded Isabella and gave a standing instruction that she should obey Christopher and do whatever he wants. Isabella didn't have any words to express her helpless situation to anybody, and she was practically doing whatever Christopher wanted. Christopher exploited the situation and started sexually abusing her. Christopher practically tortured Isabella and seduced her. Isabella conceived at the age of seventeen, and it ruined the entire family, and particularly Isabella's life. The failure of Josephine to understand the situation caused this debacle for the family.

Parents exercising excessive control over children under the cover of discipline make the children grow up in an environment of fright and fear and such children grow up with low self-esteem and poor decision making power.

In my practice, I have often come across parents who periodically say that they have sacrificed their entire life for the sake of the child. This may pose a big psychological burden for the children to shoulder and digest. It is always better for parents to lead by example of their own instead of preaching.

As the child is growing into an adolescent age, his thinking becomes more and more abstract. At this stage, his relationship with his peers become more prominent and important as there are physical, emotional, and other psychological changes happening, and peers will be able to relate and support in an admirable way.

Many times, there is a feeling among parents that the child likes his peers more than family. Most of the time, they chat with their friends, and they like to spend more time with their friends compared to the time they spend with the family. It is a typical prerogative that at this stage as the children learn a lot of psychological skills from the peers.

During adolescence, they are in the process of developing their identity which is different from that of parents. They are in the process of differentiation. There is a need for both togetherness and also separateness. Families which are highly enmeshed find this differentiation very difficult.

Most of the conflicts between parents and children happen during this stage. Open communication aid them to discuss this dependence versus independence. Parent need to understand their need to differentiate does not mean they are isolating their family

When the process of differentiation has happened, the individual grows as a mature, resilient, and confident adult. Differentiation depends upon the autonomy one receives in the growing years and is a direct indicator of mental health. Open communication on values and boundaries develop better clarity both among parents and child.

The basic understanding here is for the parents to accept the child's growth and accept they are growing and respect their rights to have their opinion, which may be totally different from the parents. And any friction at this stage between a parent and them would obviously lead to a lot of emotional impact and scars.

Attraction towards the opposite sex is quite normal, but the routine happening at this age would alarm the parents very much. Confusion regarding the choice of careers are also very common at this age, and the parents should not be disturbed by that fact. One major source of concern is doubts about sexuality.

An IT professional was sad and experienced feelings of loneliness. He approached therapy for his stress. In the course of counseling on deep probing, he said this stress was because he is sexually not normal and decided not to get married. He continued saying that he got into a bad habit when he was in his teens. When probed what those bad habits were, he said he masturbated. Later, he started masturbating every day. Whenever he decided not to masturbate, he had emission during sleep. This caused a lot of fear and doubts about his own sexual normalcy. During therapy, he was educated on sexuality, and when told that this was a very normal process of maturation and there was no element of abnormally in the act, he felt very relieved and relaxed. This shows that education on sex is very crucial and it can prevent a lot of issues during childhood and adolescents.

A symposium will exist in the adolescent mind to choose between dependency and autonomy. On his own, the adolescent may come back to take guidance from a parent, and many times, he feels, and his autonomy is superior to dependency and goes with his gut feeling. Fighting for autonomy from parents is very typical of this age.

Good communication is an important parenting skill. Parenting can be more enjoyable when a positive parent-child relationship is established. Whether you are parenting a toddler or a teenager, open communication is the key to building self-esteem as well as mutual respect. Let the child know that you are interested and involved and that you will help when needed.

Parents should obviously create a way for very transparent and open communication with the children at this stage of adolescence to give them the air of comfort and the feeling of freedom that will shape them well.

Omnipotent Factor of Observational Learning

"Children have never been very good at listening to their elders, but they have never failed to imitate them."

— James Baldwin

Bella, a Nigerian Chimp boy, was deserted by his parents as he was physically and mentally disabled. He was also believed to be raised by chimpanzees. He was found with a chimpanzee family in a forest in northern Nigeria. When he was first discovered, Bella was walking like a chimpanzee, using his legs and dragging his arms on the ground since all these years chimpanzees raised him. He was brought and made to stay in a dormitory along with other children. He was smashing the goods and throwing anything in hand and spoiling them. Six years later, although many of his behaviors were like the other children, he still walked like a chimpanzee. He was making typical chimpanzee noises and clapped his chopped hands over his head repeatedly.

Learning by observing the behavior of other people around works out very fine with children and also to a great extent with adolescents and adults also. Observational learning plays a very critical role in developing appropriate and inappropriate forms of behavior.

When the observed model is positively rewarded for a particular behavior, that behavior is more likely to be emulated and followed.

Lawrence and Laila had two children, Lincoln and Lenin. The younger son, Lenin, was five years old, and he was very well behaved while the elder son, Lincoln, who was nine years old, used to behave adamantly and got his way by throwing temper tantrums and being self-injurious and outrageous. The parents were yielding to his demands because of his arrogant and adamant attitude, fearing his volatile consequences. On many occasions, the younger son, Lenin, was asked to compromise. As the years passed by, Lenin observed that the maladaptive behavior of Lincoln was always rewarded more by the parents. He also followed and started resorting to a similar pattern of adamant behavior. To the child, the elder brother's behavior appeared ideal behavior as it was reinforced by the parents.

The same structure was also found in another case. Shwetha is 35 years old, and as a reaction to stress, she often gets a headache. Such episodes happen on and off. Now seeing and observing Shwetha, her eight-year-old daughter Sonia began to show similar complaints whenever she had a lot of homework had to cover a lot of portions of a subject or whenever there was excessive pressure to study.

She had just imbibed the behavior of the mother by constantly observing her. Researches have shown that not only physical symptoms but even extreme self-injurious behavior like suicide also runs in families as it is a coping mechanism to extreme stress which is modeled from the family.

Observational learning describes the process of learning through watching others, retaining the information, and then later replicating the behaviors that were observed. However, a great deal of learning happens indirectly. For example, think of how a child watches his parents wave at one another and then imitates these actions himself. A tremendous amount of learning happens through this process of watching and imitating others.

Observational learning also plays an important role in the socialization process as children learn how to behave and respond to others by observing how their parents and other caregivers interact with each other and with other people.

Psychologist, Albert Bandura, is the researcher perhaps most often identified with learning through observation. He and other researchers have demonstrated that we are naturally inclined to engage in observational learning.

Albert Bandura, the behavior scientist, conducted a lab experiment with two groups of children. One group watched the video where the model is behaving aggressively with the Bobo doll, a doll which gets up itself in standing position when knocked. This group of children were attacking and punching the doll rudely and also hitting the doll with a hammer brutally. The second group of children watched the video of the model playing normally with the doll.

In this famous Bobo doll experiment, Bandura demonstrated that young children would imitate the violent and aggressive actions of an adult model. In the experiment, children observed a film in which an adult repeatedly hit a large, inflatable balloon doll. After viewing the film clip, children were allowed to play in a room with a real Bobo doll just like the one they saw in the film.

What Bandura found was that children were more likely to imitate the adult's violent actions when the adult was actually rewarded for their violent actions.

The children who saw film clips in which the adult was punished for this aggressive behavior were less likely to repeat the behaviors later on.

According to Bandura's research, there are a number of factors that increase the likelihood that a behavior will be imitated. We are more likely to imitate people we perceive as warm and nurturing and people who receive rewards for their behavior. When you have been rewarded for imitating the behavior in the past, we lack confidence in our own knowledge or abilities.

Relating the famous Bobo doll experiment, we can observe children who are hitting their teddy bear with the belt. Such reactions should be more alarming for parents.

The same principle was seen when a lady police inspector, Fatima, brought her eleven-year-old son, Akhtar, for therapy complaining that whenever she corrected his actions or whenever she tried to stop what Akhtar was doing, he started hitting her. When I discussed this with the child, on probing, he said that Fatima beats him blue and black and is treating him like a thief for even small mistakes. As he grew, he picked up the habit of hitting the same way the mother hit him.

I also came across a similar case of a parent who brought her child saying that when somebody stops his activity, he bangs himself on the wall. An in-depth discussion with the parents showed that the child's father had a similar Behavior , whenever he is frustrated or whenever he is angry or furious about something.

Children closely and keenly observe their parent's behavior. When the child finds a difference in what the parents say and what they do, they obviously try to follow what the parents do.

On the other hand, very positive behaviors like courtesy, honesty, kindness are also observed and learned from the near and dear. Fear also gets instilled in children from parents through observations. The child observes where the parents panic and follow the same. A daughter picks up the fear towards cockroaches and lizards by observing her mother fear them.

Studies have categorically revealed that when smoking was shown in the movies earlier, more number of teens resorted to smoking as they saw their hero being admired for popular behavior. Among teens and adolescence, learning by observing their peers is certainly more in both positive and negative behavior.

Children's Basic School of Learning are Parents

Children learn by observing parents only. In a family, where lying, bluffing, and stealing is a regular practice, children very easily pick up these practices. Rather they even try to justify what they do. If the parents just preach and they do not practice, there is absolutely no chance or avenue for the children to listen to their advice. Many times, the maladaptive influence of peers and the environment takes place since there is no clear value system embedded in the child as it is growing. The best way for parents or elders to teach worthy values to children is to be an example by practicing those values. When this is done, it is certain that the children would emulate the elders.

A mother was telling the child to be truthful and confident. But her circumstances compelled her to be hidden in the house when she has to avoid a person to whom she has to give the money. She asks the child to lie to the person who knocks the door demanding the repayment of the money. Such incidents are enough for children to forget and disrespect all the values the elders would have taught them.

Simple things like, "Do not tell daddy what we did," or "Do not tell teacher what is happening at home and who is doing the homework for you," enters the mind of the child, who comes to a conclusion that lying is not a wrong thing. Parents should always be conscious of the pair of little eyes that are always watching them.

Parents who are non-expressive, non-empathetic, and lacking in warmth and compassion pass on similar behavior to the children. Parents are highly influential in the life of a child, and they are strong models available to the child in the formative years. Children observe how adults around them emotionally conduct themselves in various situations and learn the same.

Giving Fine Values in Formative Years

A psychologist friend of mine asked her child to clearly list out the various values of life which he feels are very essential. She gave him a list of values like humility, generosity, gratitude, responsibility, honesty, and love, etc. She further asked him what were the two values he would like to practice in life and also in what all situations he could follow them. She encouraged the child when she found him practicing it.

Again, she supported him to review all those values of life he was practicing. After a period of time, the values etched a deep root in the child's brain, and it became the core strength which defined his behavior. As he was getting stronger and clearer in life, the great thing was he chose peers who were matching his wavelength and moved with them and developed a friendship with them.

When these values are given to the child in the formative years, the parent doesn't have to physically be there to guide the child, his values will give him guidance in different situations in his life. When this value system is not properly developed, an individual becomes highly vulnerable, and the risk of his getting influenced by maladaptive behavior would happen. As the child develops to become an adolescent, the values of the peer group become increasingly important. The adolescent tries to put the values he had from parents and the peers into a single picture. Studies reveal that adolescents retain their parent's values on crucial issues and their peer's values on certain superficial issues.

A politician had brought his son who is studying in his plus two with science as the main subject. His aspiration was to become a doctor. But the father implied that he had fared very well in education in his primary school days, and when he entered the senior classes, he was not concentrating that much on academics. He was not spending time on academics as he grew up.

During counseling, the son revealed that he had seen his father collecting money for getting the medical seat, that too from students who have not even fared well in the exams. This act of the father planted the seed in the brain of the son. His father was powerful and getting the medical seat may not be a problem for him. This made him lose motivation for academics.

Gratitude is another crucial value. Many times, children take for granted the efforts made by a loved one and this habit may extend to adulthood. Gratitude helps to magnify positive emotions.

Research has shown that it plays a vital role in an adult's well-being and success. It is a strong indicator of mental well-being. When we start to recognize that others are contributing to making our life worthwhile, the way we see ourselves and others is transformed.

Results suggest that it helps maintain and strengthen supportive relationships. When people whose sense of gratitude is higher when compared to those who are lower, it was found that the first group is happier, optimistic, and have better social connectedness and are more satisfied in general. It is very crucial to impart this value when the child is small.

One parent has this as a fun activity. They had a piggy bank, and all the members of the family wrote on a slip of a paper incidents which made them feel good.

They allotted a time of the week when they sat together and took out those slips and read them aloud. Here the child starts giving his attention to the very small things and never took anybody's efforts for granted. It is nothing but consciously drawing their attention and being grateful to people and this later extends to life in general.

Parental beliefs – The Pattern Setter For Children Growth

The overall personality of parents has an impact on a child's personality. Parents have certain beliefs about themselves, about the world, and this colors their beliefs about parenting, which in turn, has an outcome on the child's belief about the parent, about himself, and his world.

Children related the kind of experience they had with their parents to the outside world. Their perception of their parents spread to the perception of the world.

If the parent has a strong belief that he is superior to the child and has to control the child, this belief will directly show in the parent's behavior in the form of demanding obedience, controlling the child's social life, over protecting the child, and acting self-righteous. Here, the impact on the child can be varied like he may rebel from dominance, hiding true feeling leading to lying and feeling inadequacy and anxiety.

A girl was doing her first year in college. Her parents were both doctors. She was completely insulated from the outside world in the sense that she was picked up and dropped by one of the parents. Even if she had to buy stationary, her father accompanied her. She was not allowed to make decisions for herself regarding her social life, further studies, and her career.

Her father strongly felt that he'll be the best decision making authority in her life and that he knows what is right for her life. Her parents also injected the feeling in her that it is because of her they have sacrificed their careers and settled for less. Paradoxically, the father feels that she is not competent and adequate in dealing with issues in her life. Due to this kind of control, the daughter too felt that she was not capable.

On the other hand, parents believe that the child is equal, and can make their own decisions. These parents would encourage freedom and the independence of the child and allow them to make their own decisions. The parents would also allow them to make their own choices and motivate them to take up responsibilities of their own.

The child who is brought up in such an atmosphere and ambiance would feel more confident. The impact of parents believing in them would make them strong, sturdy, more resourceful, and highly responsible. The child would experience a feeling of equality in every relationship.

Many times, parent set precise, perfect standards, and that will show in their behavior in the form of finding faults, and pushing the child to worry about the opinions of all others around him. In this case, either the child would also become a perfectionist or totally topsy-turvy, and would be totally discouraged and dejected with the worry that he is not able to reach the expectations of the perfectionist father. Research has shown that these parenting beliefs lead to anxiety proneness in the child. Fear of criticism, concern about others approval, the inability to tolerate setbacks is higher among these children.

Roshima was doing her schooling, and her mother was in a job which required very long working hours. The mother used to come home late in the evenings. Most of her conversations after she came back from office would be advising Roshima about keeping the house clean and being critical about the same. The moment she returned from the office, her eyes would roll around the house to see if there is any dirt or imperfections. Over a period of time, Roshima started developing palpitations and discomfort when it was time for the mother to come home. The mother was alarmed and was shocked to see the daughter wake up at midnight in her sleep and take the broom to clean the house.

If the parent is tolerant of imperfections, he will set very realistic standards. He would also strive along with the child to make him focus on his strengths without any fear or discontent. As the child may not have a fear of mistakes, he would exert more efforts to innovate and improvise newer things.

If the parent is overconcerned about fairness with a lot of strings attached, generally, the child would lose trust. The child would certainly believe that all the elders have hidden motives in their plans while giving anything to others. He may even feel exploited and may develop the same you-owe-me belief towards people in their life. The child may doubt the intentions of people who want to support him.

When no strings are attached, the child respects themselves and others, and the result is increased social feelings and developing trust in all others.

Sometimes, parents without knowing the emotional burden, are putting making children rehearse the things they have done to make the child's life better multiple times. They convey a message that I have done these things, and now it is your turn to do for us. The child starts perceiving their love as conditioned. This may reflect in his trust in relationships with others.

Seetha was working as a translator in a leading company. She decided to give up her job when her daughter entered the tenth standard. Although the decision was hers, she felt a void when not going for a job. This led to her complaining to her daughter that it is because of her that she had to leave her job. This caused irritability within the child to the extent of affecting her academics.

Take the case of a couple, Latha and Srinivasan. There was a lot of conflict and incompatibility in the relationship. Whenever there was a conversation between them, there was plenty of blame involved. He blamed her parents, and she used abusive words to address his parents. Conversations turned to dirty fights. Each parent used this child for venting out their feelings, and over a period of time, they stopped talking to each other. Whenever they wanted to convey a message to one another, they made use of the child. Although they felt it was a very convenient setup as this avoided a lot of ill feelings, they were not aware of the kind of emotional burden the child was bearing on her little shoulders due to this.

Many times, children who are brought for therapy for emotional issues are found having a lot of emotional burden due to parental incompatibility.

Another common belief of parents is that they don't count as their children are important. Such parents tend to overindulge the child's actions. They yield to the pressures of the child and feel guilty of saying NO to the child. This behavior of the parents makes the child more self-centered, leading to poor social contacts. He may not respect others and always expects to receive things.

But if parents know when to say NO, that would mold the child properly, and in the long run, that would encourage mutual respect and contributions from the child also. Such children would have fine social relationships. They would have strong self-respect, and they would also respect the rights of all others who are concerned with them. Setting the limit and giving limited choices will help the child.

Over Involved and Uninvolved Parenting – the Wide Difference in Children Growth

Over-involved parenting makes the child become too dependent, and his decision making, thinking skills, and the coping mechanism will remain dormant. Similarly, uninvolved parenting leads to feelings of neglect and poor social connectivity. Here, in uninvolved parenting, parents have no emotional involvement with the children.

Although the child's basic needs like food, education, and shelter are met, the psychological parameters remain untouched and unfulfilled. Here, warmth, love, and a connection is missing. Parents may be over-involved in their own issues and problems. Research has shown that children of uninvolved parents reflect in areas such as social skills and academic performance. These children show a deficit in cognitive, emotional, and social skills.

Due to the lack of emotional responsiveness from parents, these children have difficulties forming emotional attachments later in life. A complete lack of boundaries at home makes it difficult to learn appropriate behavior in school and other social situations. In most of the cases, the child who is brought up by uninvolved parents grows up to be cold, impersonal, detached, and shut down.

Rekha lost her husband. She has one daughter and one son who were doing their schooling. She was lost so much in her grief that she was emotionally completely disconnected from children. Her elder sister, who provided emotional solace to her, lived in the neighborhood. Whenever the children came home from school, she would not be at home, and there would be nothing for the children to eat when they were hungry.

Rekha would not notice when her child was sick. This led to an emotional void in the children. Her son, who was in the seventh started, started staying away from home after school. Her daughter, who was in the ninth standard, fell in love with a man who was married and had children. When one of her neighbors brought this to the notice of Rekha, she was shocked.

Rekha was so lost in her own issues that the emotional needs of children were completely ignored. Children who are brought up in such an emotionally disconnected environment face a lot of emotional, social, and psychological issues.

Similar problems happen when the child is brought up in an over-involved family. Anita, a ten-year-old kid, was very much interested in tennis, and she showed glimpses of an analytical mind while playing. She was invariably awarded for her remarkable tennis skills during her school days. Having observed this, her father, Gopichandran, decided to make her a tennis star. He arranged for regular coaching in the tennis academy of the coach, Mr. Anand Vijay.

Gopichandran took a lot of initiative in seeing that her tennis coaching goes excellently. Even the coach, Anand Vijay, offered his best to coach Anita. Gopi was even neglecting his office work for the sake of Anita's tennis coaching, and he went to the extent of monitoring her lessons every day. He quite often reminded Anita that his only dream is to see her as a national star in tennis.

This puts a lot of pressure on Anita as she felt her father would be disappointed if she is not able to shine as a good tennis player. But Gopi spent a lot of money on her, and Anita's mother, Gajalakshmi, also had expectations and it added all the more tension to Anita while playing. She was not able to take it as motivation by parents, but on the other hand, she was taking it as an unnecessary burden.

Whatever was once a passion for Anita became a trouble, and a burden for her as her parents and her coach were expecting a lot from her. Trying to perform more to win every match, she made a lot of silly mistakes on the court, and she was frequently getting defeated, even in games against beginners despite getting training for two or more years.

Anita felt she was responsible for making her parents glad and achieving their ambition of becoming a tennis star. But things were working out negatively for Anita as she was not able to concentrate on the game and on training. To add to this failure, she was also disconnected from her friends of the same age, and she was feeling deprived of her own likes and dislikes. Her interest went awry. Her identity was stolen, and her growth was obstructed. This resulted in low self-esteem for Anita, and it also got spread into her academics.

There was a big hue and cry within her for not reaching the expectations of her parents, and in the process, she was losing herself totally.

Anita could not vent out her real feelings as children have a limited ability to articulate. They have difficulties expressing their feelings. Suppressed feelings among children can be emotional, physical, or sexual abuse or it can be due to a cold parental attitude.

These feelings, when not properly understood and addressed, can lead to emotional and behavioral problems. The emotions which are unresolved and unexpressed, exhibit themselves in an unhealthy way. A close discussion with children having behavioral issues like stammering, bedwetting, temper tantrums shows this.

In many cases, allowing children to simply talk without judgment has a therapeutic value. One parent said, "I spend quality time on a regular basis with my child." When asked how he does that, he replied that he advises the child to be more successful, concentrate on his academics, and to be honest. When asked the child about the way the parent and the child spend time, the child expressed that the parent involves him in a boring discussion on a regular basis. In fact, when we talk about quality time, it is the fun time spent with the child, the time when they can be themselves with each other. These are the pleasant memories in the mind of a child.

Crucial Life Skills Education Make Children Confident

"Where parents do too much for their children, the children will not do much for themselves."

— Elbert Hubbard

Life skills education is very crucial, and it definitely makes children confident to face the world as they grow up. It can be cognitive skills like making decisions, facing frustrations, or it can be skills like driving, cooking, and repairing. It is very crucial to evolve overall rather than centralizing all the resources and energy only in one direction.

Allowing children to face age-appropriate frustrations and failures is an important part of their development. This makes them generate their inner potential. The world outside the home will not teach a child to handle failures gracefully. It is only the family which can enable the child to look at failures and drawbacks in a healthy perspective.

Narendran, an entrepreneur, suffered a lot due to financial hardships. He has come up in life due to his own hard work and struggles. He was married now and had a child who was only a few months old. In the course of the conversation, he narrated that he still wanted to work hard and provide all the comforts and luxury for his son. He does not want his son to struggle the way he did.

Narendran has decided to suffer to earn all the luxuries for the child. In the process, he is failing to live for himself. At the same time, he is thwarting the psychological growth of the child by providing him with everything. A healthy dose of pain is required to strengthen the child mentally and spiritually. When the child is deprived of it, it causes him to disconnect from the realities of the world.

Allowing children to face failures serves as psychological strengthening. The happiness and boost that comes by solving the problem themselves and facing the situation themselves are very healthy.

I have come across people who, as a child, were successful in every parameter. When such children face failures later in their life like a failure in love, in a relationship, or a career, they find it difficult or even impossible to accept that they get depressed. When parents accept the child's failure as much as his success, the child will learn to accept life as it comes.

A very important and essential part of parenting is to see the inner potential of the child which he is born with and provide a fertile environment for growth, rather than utilize children as vehicles to fulfill their dreams.

Real-time learning is when children learn from the inside out. For example, a child asks a question out of curiosity, rather than giving the answer, allowing him to contemplate an answer of his own to see if he could arrive at his own solutions. To trigger their thinking power, parents can, in turn, ask him, "Why do you think like that? What do you think is the right way to work out this?"

Giving them a hypothetical scenario and ask them what they think should be done, allowing and motivating them to generate alternatives.

Parents should be a co-creator rather than being the sole creator

A parent can be a co-creator rather than the sole creator of the child's thinking pattern. What if a child lacks information and knowledge. Impart this to them but allow them to seek their own answers rather than preaching to them like sage.

A close friend of mine has a daughter who is studying +2. She once told her mother her friends are going to a pub and she wanted to experiment with alcohol.

My friend, on listening to this, after thinking for a while, told the daughter that before taking the discussion further she would like to take the daughter to few places. She took her to an orphanage where the children had been deserted by their parents due to alcoholism. She also took her daughter to the cancer wards of a hospital where the patients were suffering various types of cancers due to the uncontrolled consumption of alcohol.

Finally, she took the daughter to de-addiction centers to let her know how the relatives of alcoholics suffer to bring them back to a normal life. After taking her daughter to all these places, she spoke to the daughter and asked her to decide by herself.

The belief that the child has the potential to make his decisions enhances the confidence level of both the parent and the child.

Understanding the right time to detach the umbilical cord

A child is born with power and parents take up the power since the child is very small. As the child grows up, the parents need to release the power and allow him to make age-appropriate decisions and do things on his own. What Dr. Swaminathan terms the 'severing of the umbilical cord' is essential for the growth of both the parent and the child. This will allow the child to grow as a self-sufficient individual. As the child is growing, he is striving towards independence to become efficient in taking responsibility and evolving as an individual entity.

Many times, one of the parents gives up all their other recreations, socializing, and career to bring up the child. This may lead to the parents overindulging in a child's life leading to severe frustration in both the parent and the child.

A child who was born after fifteen years of marriage was highly pampered and not allowed to do any work. He was not allowed to go alone, ride a bicycle, and not even allowed to cross the road.

The mother bathed him and fed him till high school. Although the child's intelligent quotient was superior, his skill development is retarded as he is not allowed to do things for himself and has not learned those skills. Many times, a parent's own fears and insecurities stand in the way of the child's overall development.

> *"The most important thing that parents can teach their children is how to get along without them."*
>
> *– Frank A. Clark*

As parents, sometimes we overdo what we expected our parents to do but have failed to do. A father, during his childhood, was longing to continue his studies. But his father burnt all the books and chased him to go and earn at that young age itself. Now when his child was growing, he bombards them with opportunities which actually this child is not looking for.

He is a different child, and his requirements are different. This child is a different person altogether and will develop into a different entity. The role of a parent is to provide a conducive environment which supports growth. Healthy parenting leads to growth and the liberation of children and the growth and the liberation of the parents too. The goal of parenting is to move children from dependence to independence.

Rotter's principle of locus of control and the remarkable power of it

Locus of control is a very important principle originated by Julian Rotter. People tend to believe that that life control resides internally within them or externally on outside factors. An individual with an external locus of control perceive things are happening to them, or things are being done to them.

This perception makes them more passive and accepting. When they succeed or fail, they attribute it to outside factors rather themselves. They strongly believe that others have control over them and they have nothing to do about it. People with a high internal locus of control believe in their ability to control themselves and influence the world around them. They see their future as being in their own hands, and it is their own choices which leads to success or failure.

People with an internal locus of control believe in their ability to control their behavior all the time. A strong belief is, I am responsible for my life, and I have complete control over my behavior. Generally, people are in between these two categories, but we come across people with a very strong orientation towards one.

An individual with an external locus of control will have explanation and excuses such as, I am drinking alcohol because things are not going good, and my friends are compelling me. I am getting angry because he or she made me get angry. I am a failure because of the educational system. I am successful because of luck. Here, they do not take responsibility for both the good and bad happenings in their life. Fears, helplessness, and depression are also very common in these people. On the contrary, people with a high internal locus of control believe that my life is in my hand, and I can change situations in my life. My success or failure is a by-product of my efforts, my emotions and my behavior are mine and completely under my control.

Relationships are more satisfying to people with an internal locus of control. They do not expect others or situations should change, rather they take responsibility for themselves.

How do people develop an internal or an external locus of control? Parenting plays a vital role. When parents safely hand over the power to the child by allowing the child to decide under their safe guidance, the child, as he grows, begins to believe that the consequences are a result of his efforts and his actions. When things go wrong, they believe that it is still under their control to change the situation and also their reaction to the situation. Hence, they grow up more resilient and responsible. A sense of power and feeling capable is a direct indicator of an internal locus of control.

Feeling capable and valuable is the bottom line for good mental health, and it is a direct product of parental love and acceptance. When a child feels valued, then he'll value everything related to him, his health, his time, and relationships.

Carry Home Message
From the Chapter

Your behavior is highly influential to your child.

Sow the seed of fine values and release them to face the world.

Children grow into strong adults when allowed to face what life bestows upon them, both successes and failures, pleasure and pain.

PART - 5

DEALING WITH EMOTIONS

Emotional Hijacking

At some time or the other in our life, we remember we said harsh words during fights. When the battle is over, although we say we didn't mean what we said, the other party is convinced that it was meant to hurt.

Moorthy was an employee in a private firm. During a feedback meeting with a higher official, Moorthy felt highly offended when his flaws were pointed out. He, in a rage, said harsh words. Getting hostile, he uttered that he is kicking the job and impulsively submitted his resignation.

In this case, we observe that the emotional part of the brain has completely taken up logical, rational thinking. This primitive part reacts with intense emotions without logical thinking about the consequences.

Take the case of Ravi, who was feeling very guilty for hitting his father when he saw his father use abusive words towards his mother.

My experience with prisoners is similar. Babu was sentenced to life imprisonment. He used to be on frequent business tours. Once, when he returned home, he discovered his wife with his friend. He immediately took a chopping knife and killed both of them. He has two small children, and now he feels that he could have handled the situation in a better way.

The initial and immediate response to such a situation is from a part of the brain named amygdala and is a very primitive response to a threat. The threat can be imagined or real, to the life or to the ego.

After a gap, when the rational brain, which is the seat of thinking and judgment, understands that the response was irrational, hasty, and damaging, there is a lot of regret.

Take the case of a father who hit his son watching pornography. Later, when the son ran away from home, he realized that it was the curiosity of adolescence, and it could have been dealt with in a better way.

Many times, decisions made like this can ruin life and ruin relationships.

During intense anger, as an intense emotional response, I have seen people attempting suicide and later pleading with doctors to save them.

Due to this, the gap between stimuli and response is very healthy. It is nothing but consciously borrowing time from yourself so that you are in your senses when you respond.

Emotional Haste

Similar to emotional hijacking is another phenomenon, which takes away mental harmony and which is more chronic in action. This is emotional haste.

I often hear people say that when they are on duty, they dream of a vacation. When they are on vacation, they think about forthcoming meetings and deadlines. When we are in the present, we worry about the future. When we are in the future, we are still worrying about the future and finally regret having not lived our life.

Generally, a numb blindness occurs when we rush through our lives. We get trapped in the ongoing chatter which is happening in the mind. There is always a commentary running in the mind, the commentary about a scenario which has not happened. This commentary prevents us from listening to our own feelings. This tearing apart takes away all the attention, and we miss the pleasure, safety, and harmony of the moment.

We rush and run to complete the target, to reach the destination. We are made to believe by ourselves and by others that doing many tasks at a time is a skill. We train our mind to feel guilty when we rest and relax, when we take a break from routine, and when we slow down.

On the contrary, there are people who enjoy the very process more than the goal. They are more still, calm and relaxed. When such a person goes for a vacation, he would have enjoyed the very process of preparation, the process of the journey, and the tiny joys which come along the journey. This attitude of enjoying the process when spread to the entire life, life becomes more happy and fulfilling.

The former approach to life leads to many health hazards both physical and psychological. Most of the problems such as digestive issues, sleep disturbances, sexual dysfunctions, anxiety, generalized body pain, and forgetfulness are directly related to this haste.

John was working in a private organization. He was a typical hasty type, whose mind ran in the distant future. He sought something or the other to worry about. This started affecting his intimate relationships after his marriage. When he was with his wife, the moment his mind moved into haste and worry, he switched off and could not proceed sexually. When his mind was busy running in the future and catastrophizing it, he could not stay in the present and enjoy the very process which was a major characteristic of sexual performance and gratification.

Similar is a case of an employee. Whenever there were deadlines, her existing anxiety shot up, and she felt a band around her chest and a tingling sensation. This would be followed by a fear that she was going to collapse. Although all physiological causes were ruled out, she still continued to have them.

SIMPLE COPING FOR EMOTIONAL HIJACK AND EMOTIONAL HASTE

Create a life that feels good on the inside, not one that just looks good on the outside.

Mindful Savoring

A bird mindfully builds the nest with all its mental resources focused on the task, enjoying the pleasure of making the nest. A cow savors the grass mindfully. The squirrel eating a piece of grain puts all its attention on it as if that is the only task it has on the earth at present. These are nothing but meditating on a day to day activity, just slowing down, taking a pause, and experiencing the activity.

Life has many pleasures, overlooking and moving quickly to something else is an automatic and easy response. When a child is born, we are logically driven to grow him, and to make him complete grade after grade. We fail to enjoy those moments which were very tiny but could have been fun-filled and full of happiness. We forget to enjoy the small happiness which comes to us.

People generally believe that post-retirement, when all their responsibilities are over, they will spend time on themselves to travel, and experience fun activities, but they realize later that they have not taught themselves to seek pleasure at all. They have just driven themselves to complete one thing after the other. This has now become habitual.

The human mind is such that we exaggerate, in our mind, all of the negative things which come our way. We linger on them in such a way that our mind becomes an addict to negativity and starts searching for things to worry and brood about. We take positive things for granted. We passively wait for positive experiences and actively search for negative experiences. Over a period of time, this becomes so habitual that we foresee all the pleasurable moments and we forget to cherish happy moments and spontaneously notice and worry about unhappy moments.

Dr. Fred Bryant, a professor at Loyola University, proposed the concept of mindful savoring. He showed that by taking time and spending effort to focus on positives and being attentive to your senses, your feelings, and your thoughts, you are able to experience more well-being. People who mindfully savor are happy, optimistic, and satisfied. It is not just the awareness of pleasure but also conscious attention to the experience of pleasure. It is completely absorbing the details of pleasurable feelings. It is one technique of positive psychology.

In one study, participants who were under severe stress were invited to take a few minutes once a day to relish something that they usually hurry through. It can be as simple as eating or taking a shower. They were asked to write how they felt when they savored it mindfully as compared to when they rushed through it. Results showed that it was helpful in shedding their anxiety. The feeling of well-being was enhanced.

Savoring mindfully is highly effective when people are involved in emotional eating, compulsive overeating, binge eating, purging, and other unhealthy eating related to mental stress. It is about savoring food with intense joy. When this is done, we feel full and satisfied in just a few bites. Savoring is mindfully paying attention to a morsel of food as if you were meditating. Here, your thoughts, your feelings, and your behavior are in sync with each other.

The simple technique of taking a small pause amidst a hectic day and mindfully savoring the pause, experiencing the stillness and silence within oneself, and the peacefulness between the breath, helps to rejuvenate and recharge one's mental batteries.

This technique I frequently use with my clients who come with memory issues such as forgetting where the key or wallet was kept. What happens is the mind is moving fast in multiple directions, and the activity, for example where the key was kept was not registered by the mind. When mindful savoring was practiced for any one or two activities, it spread to more and more activities over a period of time and a generalized feeling of focus, harmony, and well-being sets in.

One of my clients, when asked to choose any one activity, chose savoring a shower mindfully. He said it was more of a pleasurable meditation. He said he kept all the distraction away, and he cherished the dropping of water on the body, the water traveling down, and enjoyed the feel of it. He consciously exaggerated this feeling in his mind. He made a note of his feelings, pre and post showering. This mindful showering not only cleans the body but also relaxed the mind.

"Set peace of mind as your highest goal and organize your life around it."

— Brian Tracy

Cognitive Flexibility – A Coping Strategy

"Meanings are not determined by situations, but we determine ourselves by the meanings we give to situations."

— Alfred Adler

Cognitive flexibility is another coping ability of people in various situations. Cognitive flexibility is to switch thinking as an adaptation to the situation's requirement.

Cognitive flexibility can be seen from a variety of viewpoints. A synthesized research definition of cognitive flexibility is a switch in thinking, whether that is specifically based on a switch in rules or broadly based on a need to switch one's previous beliefs or thoughts to new situations. As such, if one is able to overcome previously held beliefs or habits in demand of the new situation, then they would be considered cognitively flexible. Cognitive flexibility has been defined as having the understanding and awareness of all possible options and alternatives simultaneously within any given situation.

Research reveals that when cognitive flexibility is high, our acceptance of differences in terms of relationships, religion, and culture, the living conditions are better. They are able to maintain a work-life balance. It is like attaching a gear to your beliefs and behavior. Researches have shown that cognitive flexibility is a direct indicator of marital harmony and couple compatibility. People low on cognitive flexibility find great difficulty in adapting to change and they resist novel situation that are behavioral, psychological, environmental, and technological.

Intrapersonal communication

A lot has been discussed about interpersonal communication, which is how we communicate to people around us. Much more than interacting with others, it is our interactions with our own selves. Throughout the day, we keep talking to ourselves about people, situations, and ourselves. Our thoughts are nothing but self-statements or self-talk. It is the quality of our self-talk which decides our relationship with ourselves with others, and our perception of the world and its challenges.

When things are repeated, it becomes automatic. For example, washing utensils, driving, cooking when done for years, become automatic. Similarly, some kind of self-talk over and over, again and again, becomes so automatic and a strong pattern is formed in the mind.

The quality of what you say to yourself decides the quality of your mood. When an object is rubbed constantly against a particular surface, a clear pathway is formed. Similarly, the same kind of pathway is formed and created by constant self-talk. And it is quite natural, that it becomes effortless and automatic.

The self-talk which shapes individuality

I have come across my clients narrating some type of problems happening in their lives over years. Similar conflicts are happening in different relationships. A lady having fights with a neighbor shifts her house, and again starts similar fights with the new neighbor in the new locality. Sometimes, such people ask why does this only happen to me always. Sometimes, they have difficulty in a relationship. Somehow they come out of a problematic relationship to enter into a new relationship with a new person. But the paradox is they again face the same type of difficulty in the new relationship.

Psychotherapy says whatever self-statements we make leads to our feelings in a particular way. When we make harmonious self-statements about something in our mind, our feeling is harmonious. When we make critical self-statements, we feel stressed. Our mood, in general, is decided by how we have trained our mind to talk to ourselves about the world around us, about people, and about setbacks. Over a period of time, it become a habit and automatic.

Most of the time, our thought patterns are as predictable to others as they are observing us from time to time. As we go through our moods, they see the change and understand our thought patterns. To be consciously aware of our pattern of these self-statements and the resulting feelings are very crucial for mental balance and harmony. To be consciously aware of our own pattern of these self-talks is very indispensable for us as this may lead us to stress.

The way we speak to ourselves is what we hear from parents, people around, our past experiences, our beliefs and values. Each individual behaves differently in different situation. This behavior depends on what meaning we have given to this situation in our mind.

Dr. Richard Lazarus says, "Stress resides neither in the person nor in the situation. An individual's views, perceptions, belief, and expectation play a large role in whether the event is stressful. The pattern of self-talk will largely decide whether we perceive the situation stressful."

For example, two people were traveling in a train which got delayed. One person calmly opens his book, starts doing some work and remains relaxed whereas the other person gets restless, shouts, and fumes. The same event of a train delay evokes different responses.

One housewife may become agitated when guests are expected to visit their home. But another housewife in a similar situation may be calm in handling the situation.

In both these examples, the first persons referred to have fixed beliefs. People have rigid and fixed ideas such as the trains should to be on time, children should study well, the house should be spic and span, and I should be liked by everyone. These shoulds and musts in the mind take away the flexible view. The more our beliefs are fixed, the more our self-talks would be fixed, leading to stress.

For example, all of us invariably anticipate our surroundings to be clean. But if your beliefs about cleanliness are fixed, a little dust is enough to make you restless. Similarly, if your beliefs about your child are fixed; you strongly believe he should study well, should be well behaved, and should be disciplined. Even if a slight deviation happens from any one of these, it will terribly disturb you excessively. The first step in the management of emotions and stress is to be more flexible with these beliefs, which in turn flex our self- talks, leading to mental harmony.

"Be miserable. Or motivate yourself. Whatever has to be done, it's always your choice."

— Wayne Dyer

Alternate Self-talk for Harmony to Prevail

> *"Your greatest weapon against stress is the ability to choose one thought over another."*
>
> **— William James**

To be conscious of your self-talk is to catch yourself whenever you are feeling stressed. Ask yourself what you told yourself about the situation. Look for alternative self-talk. Subtly rephrase the situation in your mind using alternative self-talk. When we change the self-talk, our feelings also change. Consciously doing this every time helps us to keep harmony within ourselves.

When we say alternative self-talk, we are not faking ourselves, but we are talking about more realistic self-talk. For example, after a break up in a relationship, you don't tell yourself it is okay, it doesn't affect me. You tell your own self, something like - you know it is going to be difficult, and you will take some time to come out of it. You have coped up with failures in the past and will also deal with it. It sounds very realistic, and in fact, it is an honest truth.

Here, without just telling yourself about your problems and its awful impact, you move on to flex your beliefs and alter your self-talk.

Whenever you experience extreme emotions that means your self-statement are unrealistic and very rigid. Continue asking yourself in every stressful situation, "Can I perceive the situation differently and rephrase it differently in my mind?"

A working mother reaches home in the evening after a tiring day, finds that things are scattered here and there, music is playing aloud, and the plates are not cleared from the table. She becomes extremely angry towards the children.

From her mood, we assess that her self-talk would have been, "My family is taking me for granted. Nobody is bothered that I got tired. Children are becoming highly undisciplined, and my parenting style is no good."

This kind of self-statement will very naturally lead to high-intensity stress. As a result, she will shout at the children, feel guilty, she will not be able to relax, and the rest of the day will be stressful.

Here, if the lady has a self-talk like, "I know the house is messy. Let me relax for some time. I need to talk with children. Let me seek the help of the children to clean up the mess after some time. The children are having good fun etc," the situation would be eased relatively.

Here, although you acknowledge the situation, you don't get disturbed in your mind, and the resulting mood will be stable.

When you consciously rephrase in your mind, ask yourself how a very emotionally stable friend of yours will perceive the same situation. How she will phrase it in her mind? Also, ask yourself how you will perceive the situation when in a more relaxed state of mind?

Carry Home Message From the Chapter

Chew small pleasures **as you steady yourself emotionally.**

What you talk within yourself decides the state of harmony or disharmony.

"All is well in my world."

— Louise Hay

Printed and bound by CPI Group (UK) Ltd, Croydon, CR0 4YY

27/10/2025

01985978-0001